The Emergence of
PEER COMPETITORS

A Framework for Analysis

Thomas S. Szayna   Daniel L. Byman

Steven C. Bankes   Derek Eaton   Seth G. Jones

Robert E. Mullins   Ian O. Lesser   William Rosenau

Prepared for the United States Army

RAND
ARROYO CENTER

D1525907

The research described in this report was sponsored by the United States Army under Contract No. DASW01-96-C-0004.

Library of Congress Cataloging-in-Publication Data

The emergence of peer competitors : a framework of analysis / Thomas Szayna ...
    [et al.].
        p. cm.
    "MR-1346."
    Includes bibliographical references.
    ISBN 0-8330-3056-6
    1. Military intelligence—United States. I. Szayna, Thomas S., [DATE]

UB251 .E47 2001
327.73—dc21

                                                                                2001048217

RAND is a nonprofit institution that helps improve policy and decisionmaking through research and analysis. RAND® is a registered trademark. RAND's publications do not necessarily reflect the opinions or policies of its research sponsors.

Cover design by Barbara Angell Caslon

Published 2001 by RAND
1700 Main Street, P.O. Box 2138, Santa Monica, CA 90407-2138
1200 South Hayes Street, Arlington, VA 22202-5050
201 North Craig Street, Suite 102, Pittsburgh, PA 15213
RAND URL: http://www.rand.org/
To order RAND documents or to obtain additional information,
contact Distribution Services: Telephone: (310) 451-7002;
Fax: (310) 451-6915; Email: order@rand.org

This report is the final product of a project entitled "Prospects for the Emergence of Peer Competitors." The project was intended to improve the understanding of Army intelligence analysts of the potential for the rise of a peer competitor to the United States and to construct a framework for thinking systematically about the emergence of such a competitor.

The report starts out by defining "peer competitor," and then builds a framework for thinking about an emergence of a peer competitor, focusing on two main elements. One element consists of the pathways that a proto-peer could possibly take to evolve into a peer and perhaps a competitor. The other element consists of an overview of the strategies available to the dominant state (the hegemon) to counter the rise of a peer. The interaction of the two, represented analytically by way of a game-theoretic interaction of the decision-making rationales, can lead to an outcome ranging anywhere from accommodation to rivalry. The report then exercises the dynamics of the framework by using exploratory modeling techniques. The modeling effort presented here is more a reasoning than a forecasting tool, but it could be further developed into an operational tool in support of intelligence analysis and decisionmaking.

The intended audience for this report is the intelligence community, though analysts and scholars involved in long-term futures assessments also should find it of interest.

The research was sponsored by the Deputy Chief of Staff for Intelligence, U.S. Army, and was conducted in the Strategy, Doctrine, and Resources Program of RAND Arroyo Center. The Arroyo Center is a federally funded research and development center sponsored by the United States Army.

For comments and further information, please contact the project leaders, Daniel Byman *(byman@rand.org)* and Thomas Szayna *(szayna@rand.org).*

For more information on RAND Arroyo Center, contact the Director of Operations (telephone 310-393-0411, extension 6500; FAX 310-451-6952; e-mail donnab@rand.org), or visit the Arroyo Center's Web site at *http://www.rand.org/organization/ard/.*

CONTENTS

FIGURES

TABLES

The United States is playing an unparalleled role in its history on the world stage. Its foes are few and weak, its allies strong and numerous. The United States has the most robust economy in the world, the dominant ideology, and a military that secures the homeland from any major conventional threat. Such a favorable situation is bound to end at some indeterminate point in the future. Though there is nothing to indicate that the situation will end in the near term, the possibility exists that the United States could be slow to recognize the rise of a state or alliance that could compete with it on equal terms (as a peer) and thus respond too late. However, moving too soon could be just as detrimental. By reacting prematurely, the United States could exhaust its resources and turn a state that might have been willing to cooperate or coexist peacefully into a competitor.

The potential emergence of a peer competitor is probably the most important long-term planning challenge for the Department of Defense. This report addresses the issue by developing a conceptual framework of how a proto-peer (meaning a state that is not yet a peer but has the potential to become one) might interact with the hegemon (the dominant global power). The central aspect of the framework is an interaction between the main strategies for power aggregation available to the proto-peer and the main strategies for countering the rise of a peer available to the hegemon. Then, using exploratory modeling techniques, the pathways of the various proto-peer and hegemon interactions are modeled to identify the specific patterns and combinations of actions that might lead to rivalries.

WHAT IS A PEER COMPETITOR, AND HOW MIGHT ONE ARISE?

For a state to be a peer, it must have more than a strong military. Its power must be multidimensional—economic, technological, intellectual, etc.—and it must be capable of harnessing these capabilities to achieve a policy goal. For a proto-peer also to be a competitor (and thus a danger), it must have the desire to challenge the status quo and the rules of the international system that are largely upheld by the United States, the current hegemon. To be a true peer, it has to be capable of challenging the hegemon on a global scale (and wish to do so), and the outcome of that challenge has to be uncertain, even if the hegemon effectively marshals its assets.

Analytically speaking, the proto-peer's problem is how to aggregate power quickly without provoking the hegemon into a response that would slow its pace of growth. A proto-peer has four main paths to becoming a peer: reform, revolution, alliance, and conquest. These terms are analytical constructs rather than conscious strategies a state might adopt on its ascent to power. A proto-peer can (and indeed is likely to) pursue more than one strategy simultaneously, but generally one will dominate. Externally focused strategies (alliance and conquest) can build power faster than internally focused ones (reform and revolution), but they are also more likely to attract the hegemon's attention and provoke a hostile response from other states. Especially when the hegemon has a preponderance of power at the global level, a proto-peer must tread carefully, since it faces a potentially devastating response that could delay or end its aspirations to become a peer.

In a **reform** strategy, the proto-peer builds power by increasing national resources, or "inputs," by such means as improving its educational base or spending more on scientific research and development efforts. This strategy is incremental and generally respects the accepted "rules" of the international system. Since this strategy is gradual, relatively predictable, and follows the existing rules, the hegemon has considerable time to respond and is unlikely to be threatened.

A **revolution** dramatically transforms a state's ability to extract resources by such means as more effective governance or substantial improvement in the country's capability to provide resources. This strategy carries with it more uncertainty but has the potential to increase a state's power greatly and relatively quickly. The unpredictability of the strategy—for revolutions often bring new governments as well as new capabilities—means that the hegemon may have less time to respond (meaning a greater sense of potential threat to the hegemon), and the hegemon needs to keep a wary eye on a proto-peer following such a strategy.

An **alliance** strategy, entailing an alliance by a proto-peer with another major state or states, clearly challenges the hegemon because it can overturn the status quo and reduce the hegemon's dominant role. An alliance has an immediate effect on power calculations, although it may take years to integrate the allies (without necessarily making them dependable). The hegemon can only see such a move as threatening.

A proto-peer can also attempt to increase its power by **conquest**, forcefully subjugating another state. Such a strategy immediately changes power calculations and represents an overt attempt to overturn the existing order. Typically, such a strategy requires large and capable military forces, both to make the conquest and to consolidate its gains. Not surprisingly, the hegemon finds this strategy highly threatening.

POSSIBLE HEGEMON RESPONSES

In analytical terms, the hegemon's problem is how to remain one for as long as possible, at an acceptable cost. A peer does not arise in a vacuum. If the hegemon sees a peer competitor emerging, it will impose additional costs upon the proto-peer to slow its growth and prevent a challenge from emerging. Imposing costs can range anywhere from punitive trade measures to outright sponsorship of internal strife. Such "conflict imposition" is a tool of the hegemon in regulating potential challenges. However, the hegemon wishes to avoid direct armed conflict because it can be expensive, may alienate allies, and can lead to overextension.

A hegemon could respond in four main ways: conciliate, co-opt, constrain, and compete. Like the proto-peer strategies, these terms are analytical constructs, and the primary difference among them is the level of conflict the hegemon imposes on the proto-peer, with conciliate representing the least conflict and compete the most. The goal is to prevent any proto-peer from metamorphosing into a "principal rival," reminiscent of the Soviet role vis-à-vis the United States during the Cold War.

The **conciliate** strategy, as its name implies, entails mostly cooperative behavior by the hegemon and is designed to increase common goals and limit friction. The hegemon expects the proto-peer to be an ally rather than a competitor as it grows in power, and its actions toward such a proto-peer are relatively free of conflict. Inherent in this strategy is the hegemon's belief that the proto-peer does not pose a fundamental threat even if it matches the hegemon's capabilities because the states have similar or compatible interests.

The **co-opt** strategy is a hedging strategy designed to increase the stake of the proto-peer in the status quo, thus reducing the motivation to change it. It is primarily a "carrots" approach, but the cooperation is more conditional than it would be in a conciliation strategy. The hegemon is willing to let the proto-peer's power rise, but only if it modifies its behavior sufficiently so that it does not threaten the international system.

If the co-opt strategy hinges on "carrots," the **constrain** strategy employs "sticks." Its goal is to delay peer status without provoking a military conflict. The hegemon concludes that the proto-peer is likely to be a competitor and, to moderate its rise to power, aims to make clear the costs of such a competition. Conflict-imposition predominates in such a strategy, although the hegemon still sees a possibility of forestalling the emergence of a long-term competitor. The hegemon can modulate its strategy, increasing the sticks if the proto-peer continues to be bellicose or adding carrots if it becomes more conciliatory.

The **compete** strategy is primarily one of conflict designed to impose costs on the proto-peer, reduce its power, and keep it from achieving peer status. Ideally the conflict is not military, but that is the ultimate risk of this strategy. Given the high costs of the compete strategy, the hegemon must conclude that competition with the proto-peer is inevitable, that this poses a fundamental threat, and that the risks of not engaging in a strategy of conflict outweigh the costs. This strategy offers little positive reinforcement, since the competition is seen in zero-sum terms. Once adopted, such a strategy may be difficult to modify or abandon.

Like the proto-peer, the hegemon can blend strategies. However, the hegemon must walk a fairly narrow line: too much conciliation can speed the growth of a competitor, and too much conflict can do the same. The time horizons associated with the strategies tend to be long, and a good deal of uncertainty surrounds all the possible choices.

THE INTERACTION OF PROTO-PEER AND HEGEMON STRATEGIES

Predicting the emergence of a peer competitor is difficult. However, aggressive proto-peer strategies of power aggregation and a hegemonic response high in conflict imposition are likely to lead to rivalry and competition. Exploratory modeling techniques presented in this report can clarify the specific patterns and combinations of strategies that might lead to rivalries. We stress, however, that the model is a reasoning tool, not a forecasting tool. It is useful for understanding the implications of decisionmaking represented in the decision rules of the framework (the two sets of strategies), though it has the potential to be developed into an operational tool.

The theoretical and modeling work leads to at least three inferences regarding the potential for emergence of a peer competitor:

* The U.S. preponderance of power makes the emergence of a peer competitor unlikely in the near future;

* The most likely route for the emergence of a peer competitor any time soon is by way of an alliance;

* Errors in a hegemon's assessment of a proto-peer are more critical than errors in a proto-peer's assessment of a hegemon.

With the predominance that the United States currently enjoys, emergence of a peer competitor stems as much from U.S. actions as from those of potential peers. The United States can either delay a peer's emergence or try to moderate its potential competitive tendencies. A potential peer has a limited number of options available to become a peer, and it faces a difficult balancing act in pursuing policies that enable it to amass power without simultaneously alarming the United States. On the other hand, the United States faces its own delicate balance between not taking an overly confrontational stance in its policies toward potential peers and avoiding any actions or inactions that might hasten the rise of a peer competitor. The role of error in long-term assessment of a potential peer can be crucial, because a miscalculation can lead to unnecessary escalation and rivalry that would be difficult to undo.

ACKNOWLEDGMENTS

The authors are indebted to James Dewar (RAND), Davis Bobrow (University of Pittsburgh), Thomas McNaugher (RAND), Jeffrey Legro (University of Virginia), and Al Goldman (National Ground Intelligence Center) for reviewing an earlier version of this report. Their insightful comments have greatly improved this study. The authors also wish to thank the following personnel, either currently or formerly with the Office of the Deputy Chief of Staff for Intelligence (DCSINT), for their interest and support in the course of the project: COL Jan Karcz, COL Nicholas Szasz, Eric Kraemer, William Speer, Eric Vardac. Among RAND staff, Jeremy Shapiro was particularly helpful in the course of the project. Jerry Sollinger's advice improved the organization of this report, and Nikki Shacklett edited.

Chapter One

INTRODUCTION

After the fall of the Soviet empire and the emergence of the United States as the undisputed world leader, the United States plays a role unparalleled in its history. It has no significant opponent, is allied with most states that could compete with it on equal terms, has the largest and most robust economy in the world, has the largely dominant ideology, and has a military that provides for the security of the homeland from any major conventional threat. The dominant thinking in the U.S. defense community about the potential rise of a peer competitor is that (1) only a few states could emerge into peer competitors and still have a long way to go, and (2) there will be ample time to see such a competitor coming and to prepare for such a challenge. In the words of the former Secretary of Defense: "There is no peer competitor—and unlikely to be a peer competitor anytime soon."[1]

No matter how reasonable such views may seem, experience teaches caution. The prevailing pattern in modern history has been that, eventually, competitors to dominant states emerge, and sometimes the emergence alters the hierarchy in the international state system. Even though the current U.S. predominance has no parallels in modern history, the stakes are too high to permit complacency. Moreover, although current planning does not see a peer competitor

---

[1]Interview with the former Secretary of Defense, William Cohen, "PBS News Hour," January 10, 2001.

appearing for at least a decade, long-term assessments are murkier, with some candidates for peer-competitor status on the horizon.[2]

In the long term, the most important national security problem is the potential appearance of an adversary that challenges the United States on its own terms. Contemporary debates about weapons modernization and the possibility of "skipping a generation" in weapons technology[3] or about the proper balance in the U.S. military between long-term deterrence and near-term transformation to deal with regional conflicts and peace operations implicitly keep the emergence of a peer competitor as a fundamental rationale for guiding the development of U.S. armed forces. No issue is more fundamental to Army planning, research, development, and acquisition than the prospect of a peer competitor. The expectation or reality of such a competitor would be a watershed in the threat environment, forcing adjustments across the board in the Army's plans and policies. Since the Army's planned Objective Force is not scheduled to be in place for 20 years, thinking about the emergence of a peer competitor has direct relevance to the Army's evolution.

Given the importance of the issue, the United States must monitor closely the prospects of a peer competitor emerging and deter threats to vital U.S. interests that such an emergence would entail. Long-term intelligence assessments are key. Identifying indicators of potential peer competitors is vital to the timely allocation of the Army's modernization resources and to the development of the

---

[2]The current consensus scenario for the 2001–2025 timeframe within the Department of Defense is that the United States needs to hedge against the eventual emergence of a "military near peer," but dealing with regional competitors is the likely primary conventional military threat. Sam J. Tangredi, *All Possible Wars? Toward a Consensus View of the Future Security Environment, 2001–2025*, McNair Paper 63, Washington, D.C.: Institute for National Strategic Studies, National Defense University, 2000.

[3]The widely shared view in the U.S. defense community of an unchallenged dominant military position for the United States is often combined with a concern that the situation may not last in the long term. Thus, some have argued that to prevent a challenger in the long term, the United States should focus on extending its dominant position by pursuing aggressively emerging technologies that have the potential to thwart any potential challenger in the long term rather than expanding resources on weapons systems in the near and medium terms. The argument is that by forgoing some weapons procurement that offers mostly incremental gains, the resources should instead be concentrated on developing the potential for "breakthrough" capabilities.

Army's capabilities for deterrence and decisive force at the high end of the spectrum of future operations. Too late a commitment to programs necessary to deter an emerging peer could be disastrous. But committing resources to meet a potential peer too soon would detract from forces and readiness for other contingencies and operations.

This report addresses the issue of early identification of the circumstances for the rise of a peer competitor to the United States. The research sought to improve the Army's anticipatory skills by providing a framework, grounded in current theory about the emergence of rivalry at the apex of the international hierarchy, to aid in thinking about the interaction between a proto-peer (a state that is not yet a peer but has the potential to become one) and a hegemon (the dominant global power) that eventually might lead to competition and conflict. Under what conditions are proto-peers likely to turn into competitors? When are proto-peers more likely to accommodate rather than compete? Given the crucial role of long-term forecasts in shaping the policy toward a proto-peer, under what conditions can errors in assessment lead to hegemon policies that overemphasize conflict and may actually hasten the emergence of a peer competitor? In an overall sense, the project researchers tried to think about the emergence of a peer competitor systematically, pulling together the existing scholarly knowledge about the issue and transforming it into a tool useful for guiding policy and intelligence assessments.

The exploratory modeling effort that follows the framework is currently more a reasoning tool than a forecasting tool. The results are not empirical. Instead, the insights stem from logically deduced sets of causal statements about the structure of and processes governing the interaction between a proto-peer and the hegemon. The results and insights produced by the framework, as exercised in the modeling effort, are encouraging, and the framework and the model could be developed into an operational tool to support intelligence analysis and decisionmaking.

ORGANIZATION

Chapter Two begins by defining the peer competitor concept. The term is used primarily within the Department of Defense. The scholarly literature uses terms that approximate it but do not have the same meaning. Clarifying the concept is important because drawing on the scholarly literature has the potential to add insights to the debates within DoD on the topic of peer competitor. The chapter then elaborates four pathways that a proto-peer could take to evolve into a peer and perhaps a competitor. The chapter draws on insights from social science (political science, economics, and history). This work also builds on recent Arroyo Center research, especially an assessment of the indicators of state power in the contemporary world and an examination of the relationship between economic growth and rise of military power.[4] The goal of this chapter is to introduce the concepts and strategies that are then developed further with the exploratory model.

Chapter Three looks at the issue from the perspective of the hegemon. Since the hegemon's problem is how to remain one for as long as possible at an acceptable cost, it too has a limited number of strategies to follow. The four main strategies are based mainly on the extent of potential threat that the hegemon assesses. The differences between them lie primarily in the extent of sanctions that the hegemon might use to thwart the power growth of the proto-peer. The chapter concludes with a presentation of the concept of rivalry among the principals in the international system. Should the hegemon fail to prevent the rise of a peer, competition between such a new principal and the hegemon might result. The challenge for the intelligence community is to identify a potential peer competitor before it becomes a rival. The chapter draws on insights arising primarily from political science and, like Chapter Two, is intended to introduce concepts for the overall model.

Chapter Four presents the model. Based on the interaction of the various strategies, the authors constructed a game-theoretic representation of the rationale for decisions by both the hegemon and the proto-peer. The decision rules in the game then served as the foundation for an exploratory modeling effort. The modeling starts with the idea that projections and assessments of relative power growth

---

[4]Ashley J. Tellis, Janice Bially, Christopher Layne, and Melissa McPherson, *Measuring National Power in the Postindustrial Age*, Santa Monica, CA: RAND, MR-1110-A, 2000; Jasen Castillo, Julia Lowell, Ashley J. Tellis, Jorge Muñoz, and Benjamin Zycher, *Military Expenditures and Economic Growth*, Santa Monica, CA: RAND, MR-1112-A, 2001.

lead to strategy choices, and that the four possible strategies each side can employ interact to produce their own dynamics. The model assumes both ground truth and assessment (perception represented as ground truth and probability error). The model provides insights into the conditions that lead to competition, which attributes are pivotal, the potential policy results from different assessments, and the variation in value of intelligence assessments across alternative situations.

Chapter Five summarizes the main findings and draws out some inferences for long-term defense policies.

The report includes three appendixes. Appendix A presents the decision rules for the modeling effort, and Appendix B contains the code for the model. Appendix C provides a critical review of the literature on democratic peace (the proposition that democracies do not wage war on each other). Evidence generally supports the proposition, but enough uncertainties surround the logic behind it to warrant caution. Although the probability of a democratic peer competitor to the United States seems low, the blanket statement that such an outcome is impossible is, as yet, insupportable.

Chapter Two

THE RISE OF A PEER

WHAT IS A PEER COMPETITOR?

An initial problem in tackling the issue of a peer competitor's emergence is the term's murkiness. In defense circles, the term refers to challenges that go beyond conventional major theater wars (MTWs). The academic literature, however, does not use the term. Instead, it uses terms such as hegemon, great power, and major power, all of which overlap with the idea of a peer competitor. The diverse terminology and the different ways of thinking about peer competitors implicit in the different terms make it difficult to clarify the concept.

Thus, our first step is to clarify definitions. As the term suggests, a peer competitor has both capabilities (peer) and intentions (competitor). Both are necessary for a state to be a peer competitor. A state can be hostile to the United States but lack the capabilities to challenge it beyond a local crisis, or it can have the capabilities but not the intentions. The issue is examined in greater detail below, describing the nature of peer competitors and distinguishing them from other challenges.

A peer competitor, as the term is used here, is a state or collection of challengers with the *power* and *motivation* to confront the United States *on a global scale* in a sustained way and to a sufficient level where *the ultimate outcome of a conflict is in doubt* even if the United

States marshals its resources in an effective and timely manner.[1] We now expand on the main components of this definition.[2]

Power

Power is a necessary but not sufficient condition for a country to be a peer competitor. Without economic, political, military, and other types of power, a country can be a danger to the United States but is not likely to challenge the fundamentals of the U.S.-led international system.

This analysis draws on the framework of Ashley Tellis et al.[3] for measuring national power. As they argue, power requires sufficient "inputs," such as gross domestic product (GDP) and population. Inputs are well understood and measured by a wide range of government and nongovernment institutions. The Tellis et al. work, however, goes beyond conventional analyses and provides a framework for assessing nontraditional inputs that have greater importance in today's world, such as a country's engineering base and capacity for innovation. Selected factors identified by Tellis and his co-authors include the following:

- Technology

---

[1]This definition is similar to that used by the Department of Defense, with several minor modifications. The DoD currently defines a "global peer competitor" as a "nation or rival coalition with the motivation and capabilities to contest U.S. interests on a global scale." Our definition, in contrast, uses the phrase "collection of challengers" rather than "coalition" to reflect the possibility, albeit an unlikely one, that strong challengers could include nonstate actors as well as a coalition of states. A coalition of states, however, remains the most likely type of challenge beyond the single state. Second, our definition adds the requirement that the ultimate outcome of a challenge is in doubt even if the United States marshals its resources well. This is to emphasize the level of the challenge—it is not simply a clever regional power timing its aggression to capitalize on favorable conditions, but rather a power that, in a "fair" fight, could prevail.

[2]One of the objections that some have raised to the term "peer competitor" is that it implies a mirror-image of the adversary (MG Robert H. Scales, Jr., *Future Warfare*, Carlisle Barracks, PA: U.S. Army War College, 1999, p. 139). That point is debatable. In any event, our alternative definition is at the level of national power and intent rather than military capability, and in no way does it imply a mirror-image of the adversary.

[3]Ashley J., Tellis, Janice Bially, Christopher Layne, and Melissa McPherson, *Measuring National Power in the Postindustrial Age*, Santa Monica, CA: RAND, MR-1110-A, 2000.

- Capacity for innovation
- Skilled workers
- Education
- Capital stock
- GDP
- Energy and nonenergy resources
- Impartial legal system
- Little corruption
- State capacity for directing society if necessary
- Size and skill of military forces

But inputs alone do not determine overall power. Tellis et al. is particularly valuable in assessing transformational capacity: a government's ability to turn inputs into outputs (military power and overall influence). Transformational capacity includes not only efficient government but also an ability to harness new technologies and organizational innovation effectively and to capitalize on geopolitical changes. Transformational capacity varies tremendously by historical era. For example, what helps a government efficiently extract resources in an industrial economy may do little to exploit an information economy. Nevertheless, transformational capacity remains a crucial and often ignored link between potential and actual power.

Transformational capacity is an elusive variable, but it is vital for explaining why certain powers never achieved their potential. Czarist Russia for decades was feared as a potential dominant power in Europe, but it proved quite weak during the Crimean War and World War I. Other states habitually exceeded the level of power that their natural endowments might imply (e.g., Germany) through the skilled use of resources.

Motivations

What distinguishes a "peer" from a "peer competitor?" The answer lies in the peer's foreign policy. A peer seeks only modest or no change in the international system (the relative power status of the major states, the rules governing interaction between states, and/or the beneficiaries of those rules). A peer competitor, on the other hand, seeks to change the status quo, both to gain more power for itself and to decrease the relative power of the dominant state. To do so, the rising power must transfer relative influence in the world from the dominant power to itself. Peaceful examples include amending treaties to gain a greater voice in international decisions or modifying the trade structure to favor its citizens. More worrisome examples include attempts to conquer lost territory or to dominate neighbors. In short, a peer competitor seeks to overturn the status quo, adjusting it in its favor.

Including motives in the definition of a peer competitor raises an important question about the relation between motive and capability. Many political scientists argue that capability fosters motivation: if a power can dominate, it will. By this logic, any power that attains the GDP, population, scientific base, and other inputs along with transformational capacity will inevitably seek to rewrite the rules of the game and replace the dominant power.

But history shows tremendous variation in the behavior of rising powers. A challenge is not inevitable even when a country can afford to take on the dominant power. The United States rose in the late 19th and early 20th century without challenging directly Britain's dominant position. In the post–Cold War era, Germany and Japan became major economic powers but worked to strengthen, rather than challenge, the U.S.-led international system.

The true question is, When do a regime's motivations lead to conflict with the dominant power? Sources of hostile motivations might include a new, aggressive leadership, the emergence of nationalism, new military doctrines (such as preventive war), and other factors. Particularly common sources include acute dissatisfaction with the status quo; security concerns; leadership ambitions; and ideological imperatives. Causes often overlap in practice but are useful to separate for analytic purposes. Discussing intentions requires a distinction between states and the regimes that control them. Regimes drive motivations: the state's power and position are the material from which they build.

The hegemon, of course, can affect these causes, for good or ill. If it maintains an inflexible system inimical to the interests of the rising power, naturally the rising power may try to overturn it. More directly, the hegemon can affect a rising power's capabilities and motivations, making it less able to pose a challenge. The hegemon can threaten a potential peer, causing it to respond in self-defense.

While capabilities seldom develop quickly, motivations can change rapidly. Germany's motivations in the 19th century changed tremendously when Kaiser Wilhelm took over; Germany went from Europe's stabilizing force to its leading revisionist power. After the Bolshevik Revolution, the USSR became a major source of instability in areas adjoining it as well as in the entire world. This presents a dilemma: motivations must be addressed, for they are inherent to the definition of a peer competitor; yet analysts must recognize that motivations can change quickly.

A controversial point among international relations theorists is the extent to which democratic political systems act to curtail what otherwise is seen as a built-in propensity for conflict among states. Proponents of the "democratic peace" proposition argue that democracies do not fight each other. If the proposition is true, it greatly simplifies the entire problem of predicting the rise of a peer competitor, since it eliminates the need to consider democratic proto-peers and peers as potential competitors. Though the "democratic peace" literature is intriguing, at this stage it is too early to accept its conclusions for purposes of U.S. policy and U.S. intelligence estimates. The full argument for this assessment (including a review of the "democratic peace" literature) is presented in Appendix C.

Global Scale

A peer competitor must also have global capabilities to represent a threat to the United States. Capabilities need not be global in the sense that the competitor can act in *every* region, only in that it can act in multiple critical ones. For the purposes of this study, critical regions include industrial centers (Europe, Japan, the high-performing Asian economies), critical resource regions (the Persian Gulf), and countries/areas close to U.S. borders (Canada, Mexico, and Central America). Less important regions include the Indian subcontinent and sub-Saharan Africa, though importance changes with development, and regions that are less important now may become important in the future. Thus, a power that could strike at U.S. commerce in Asia and threaten Persian Gulf security would be able to operate on a global scale for purposes of this study. One that could threaten commerce in Asia (one critical region) and the security of several sub-Saharan African states (where U.S. interests are minimal) would not, even though it has a multiregional capability. Indeed, even a "resurgent" China that could challenge U.S. control over the sea lanes in Asia and threaten Taiwan, Korea, and Japan would not be a true peer if it could not challenge the United States elsewhere. Because of geography, a proto-peer on the Eurasian landmass probably would be in a position to threaten U.S. interests in at least two critical areas.

In cases of an emerging peer, regional primacy is often the initial goal of such a power (this is developed further in Chapter Three in the global-regional discussion of rivalries). Should such a power succeed in attaining regional primacy despite the opposition of the hegemon, then it might be in a position to attract other allies and/or weaken the hegemon's alliance system, allowing its rise to the position of a peer. In this sense, an alliance can help a regional power meet the global criterion. In World War II, for example, Japan was in essence a regional power, albeit a potent one. Its cooperation with Germany, however, enabled the combined powers to threaten U.S. interests across the globe. Possible peer alliances today include combinations of the European Union, Japan, Russia, and China.[4]

Outcome in Doubt

This final criterion emphasizes the true level of threat a peer competitor poses. Numerous analyses of Iraq and North Korea empha-

---

[4]The global criterion will be relaxed when using historical cases to illuminate our arguments. In the past, critical regions and neighboring states were almost synonyms. Even the most powerful states cared first and foremost about their neighbors (though some powers, such as the Roman Empire and Periclean Athens, depended on grain from rather distant lands, and the British Empire of course had interests throughout the globe). In most cases, however, a "peer" meant a power capable of challenging a state near its home. With the expansion of U.S. interests, however, this regional focus must expand as well.

size that surprise, weapons of mass destruction (WMD), and other factors could briefly tilt the balance in favor of these regional states, enabling them to gain a short-term advantage over the United States and its allies. Yet if the United States mobilized its power, the ultimate outcome would not be in doubt. With a true peer, however, such certainty is lacking. Defeat would be possible, as would a limited victory. For a true peer competitor, a capability to deny victory would not depend on luck but rather on the power and skill of the combatants.

THE PROTO-PEER'S STRATEGIES

A proto-peer has a limited number of strategies it can conceivably pursue to increase its power. With the primary difference among the strategies being the potential pace of growth in power, a proto-peer has four main strategies realistically available. These range from internally focused changes accompanying gradual economic growth, to a less predictable but potentially faster internally focused growth due to revolutionary changes, to an externally focused strategy emphasizing alliances with other countries, to outright aggression, intimidation, and subjugation of other countries. We refer to these four strategies as reform, revolution, alliance, and conquest, respectively. The strategies are analytical constructs, identifiable outwardly by the potential pace of power growth within them, though, at a deeper level, they may arise from any number of systemic or internal factors, such as specific regime and state characteristics, the nature of the security dilemma, or the structure of existing technology.

The relationship between the proto-peer's pace of power growth and the likelihood of a specific strategy provoking a perception of threat is largely proportional. Figure 2.1 provides a notional representation of the relationship, with the boxes representing the set of probable points of interaction between the two. The low, medium, and high marks represent the approximate range of the pace of potential growth of each strategy, with some overlap between them. The focus on power growth stems from the need for the proto-peer to catch up to the hegemon. If the proto-peer is not growing in a relative sense to the hegemon, then it is not going to become a peer. Each of the four strategies is described in detail below.

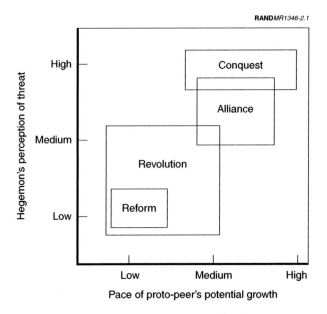

Figure 2.1—Proto-Peer's Strategies

THE REFORM STRATEGY

Characteristics

The military capabilities needed for any power to compete with the United States as a global peer generally will require an economy at least close to the United States in size, productivity, and per-capita GDP. The smaller the economy, proportionately the more resources will have to be extracted from it (or in a relatively more efficient fashion) to fuel its military capabilities. The USSR during the Cold War offers a case in point of an economy much smaller than that of the United States but a relatively similar level of military effort because of the extremely high level of militarization of the economy. In any event, for most countries today, achieving that high a level of resources will require a sustained period of robust economic growth.[5] To understand how a country might achieve that growth, this section examines both the theoretical and empirical understandings of the causes of growth.

Policies and Institutions

The question of what causes economic growth[6] is perhaps the most fundamental question of modern economics. Growth is the engine through which people are delivered from the misery of poverty and the motor behind epochal changes in the distribution of world power. Neoclassical theories emphasize accumulation of people (labor) and equipment (capital) as key ingredients. Yet hard experience shows this explanation to be inadequate. Endogenous growth theories add the accumulation of ideas (technological advance) and the skills to use them productively (human capital).[7]

The problem with these theories is not so much that they are wrong, but that they are incomplete. They tend to leave out the most interesting and meaningful variable: government policy. The question of what policy is ideal remains contentious, but there is some consensus on the broad policies and institutional configurations that have fostered growth recently.

---

[5]As a suggestive example of the time frame required, consider the following simple extrapolation of present trends. For China to reach the average per-capita GDP of the high-income countries would require 106 years of 6 percent per annum real growth (assuming the high-income countries continue growing at 2.5 percent per year, their modern historical average) and 42 years to reach $10,000 per-capita GDP in constant dollars. On a purchasing power parity basis, it would require 62 years and 22 years respectively. Calculated from 2000 World Bank Development Indicators at *http://www.worldbank.org/data/databytopic/GNPPC.pdf.*

[6]For convenience and by convention, "growth" in this section will refer to growth in per-capita GDP, unless otherwise noted.

[7]The accumulation of ideas is often expressed as total factor productivity to emphasize that the store of knowledge in a society determines how efficiently the factors of capital, labor, and human capital are combined. Seminal works in endogenous growth theory include Paul M. Romer, "Increasing Returns and Long-Run Growth," *Journal of Political Economy,* 94:5 (October 1986), pp. 1002–1037; Paul M. Romer, "Endogenous Technological Change," *Journal of Political Economy,* 98:5 (October 1990), pp. 71–102; and Gene M. Grossman and Elhanan Helpman, *Innovation and Growth in the Global Economy,* Cambridge: MIT Press, 1991.

Given that the determinants of growth vary from era to era, most experts would agree that the most important policy prescription for promoting long-term growth is flexibility. The ability to adapt to new, unforeseen challenges, rather than resting on the laurels of past success or entrenching past failures, has been and will continue to be the single most important factor in achieving sustained growth. The rare degree of flexibility in the U.S. economy would appear to be the root source of its unmatched capacity for continual renewal and probably represents its greatest relative strength.

With that caveat in mind, the following is a far from exhaustive list of the policies and institutions considered essential for growth, in roughly decreasing order of consensus:

- **Rule of law.** The greatest consensus on which policies foster growth has emerged around the need for the government to provide stable political and legal conditions.[8] "Rule of law" in the modern context refers to the institutions and mechanisms that can ensure predictable and enforceable contracts and secure property rights.

- **Education and health.** Investing in education and health is necessary to create a skilled workforce. In addition to increasing worker productivity, education and health increase growth in other ways. Better education and health care for women in particular tend to improve the educational levels and health of the next generation, to reduce fertility levels, and to reduce inequality, all of which are independently associated with long-term growth.[9] Educational levels and health indicators are viewed as the best predictors of countries poised for economic take-off.

- **Stable macroeconomic conditions.** Another area of agreement concerns the need for a stable macroeconomic framework, par-

---

[8]For a recent contribution that stresses the importance of the rule of law, see Mancur Olson, *Power and Prosperity: Outgrowing Communist and Capitalist Dictatorships,* New York: Basic Books, 2000.

[9]See Nancy Birdsall and Richard Sabot, "Inequality as a Constraint on Growth in Latin America," in Mitchell A. Seligson and John T. Passé-Smith (eds.), *Development and Underdevelopment: The Political Economy of Global Inequality,* 2nd ed., Boulder, CO: Lynne Rienner Publishers, Inc., 1998, p. 424; and World Bank, *The East Asian Miracle: Economic Growth and Public Policy,* New York: Oxford University Press, 1993.

ticularly low inflation and a reasonably stable currency exchange rate.

- **Trade openness.** While somewhat less consensus exists on the need for trade openness, most economists believe that openness to trade contributes to growth in important ways. Logically, international trade allows increased specialization and therefore efficiency, and it forces often complacent domestic firms to compete with foreign ones and therefore to become more productive. Perhaps more important for the developing world, openness gives domestic firms access to the technologies and ideas from abroad that endogenous growth theory emphasizes are so important for sustained growth.

- **Foreign investment.** One of the more controversial policies for promoting growth is the promotion of foreign investment by removing barriers to international capital flows. Free-flowing international capital allows savings anywhere to flow to the most productive investment opportunities. For borrowers, this means access to a larger pool of savings with which to finance and thus hasten their development. Recent financial crises, however, have caused some observers to resurrect the distrust of capital flows characteristic of the aftermath of the depression in the 1930s.

- **Limited government intervention.** The dismal growth performance of planned economies in recent decades[10] has created a strong consensus for limiting the role of the state in allocating investment resources. The most obvious corollary of this prescription is that governments should let markets determine prices and interest rates.

- **High investments and savings rates.** One of the defining characteristics of the recent Asian growth spurt was extremely high rates of investment, backed by high rates of savings.[11] Because investment spending is itself a component of GDP, high invest-

---

[10]Soviet growth, for example, was the worst in the world over the period 1960–1989, after controlling for investment and capital. See William Easterly and Stanley Fischer, "The Soviet Economic Decline," *World Bank Economic Review,* 9:3 (1995), pp. 341–371.

[11]In closed economies, saving equals investment by definition. International capital mobility breaks that identity by allowing investment to be financed with foreign savings. Nonetheless, national savings and investment rates remain highly correlated.

ment spending by definition boosts growth in the short term. However, diminishing marginal returns to capital mean that simply piling up machines and adding infrastructure cannot sustain growth. Misallocation of investment resources tends to foster overcapacity, speculative bubbles, and even corruption as companies and financial institutions struggle to hide the extent of the waste.

- **Democracy and freedom.** The connection between political freedom and growth is much more tenuous. A long-standing argument holds that economic and political freedoms are mutually reinforcing.[12] In this view, genuine economic freedom is impossible without the political freedom usually associated with democracy. At the same time, however, there is ample reason to expect that democracy might suppress growth by increasing the capacity of interest groups to demand inefficient government intervention in market outcomes.[13] The empirical record on the relationship between democracy and growth is similarly mixed, clouded by the problems of measuring political freedom.[14]

The Nature of the Challenge

Type of power gained. A strategy of "reform" aims at increasing exploitable resources available to regimes—the "inputs" that Tellis et al. identified as vital to power in today's world. Most obviously, successful reform increases the money and industrial base that can produce military power. In addition, reform can increase the education level of military service members, the likelihood of military and technological innovation, and other factors that increase overall power. Successful reform does not necessarily change the transformational

---

[12]Milton Friedman, *Capitalism and Freedom,* Chicago: University of Chicago Press, 1962.

[13]For an expression of the view that interest groups can slow growth, see Mancur Olson, *The Rise And Decline Of Nations: Economic Growth, Stagflation, and Social Rigidities,* New Haven: Yale University Press, 1982.

[14]For an empirical test, see Robert J. Barro, *Determinants of Economic Growth: A Cross-Country Empirical Study,* Cambridge, MA: National Bureau of Economic Research, 1996, ch. 2. Barro concludes that there is a nonlinear relationship between democracy and growth. Increased democracy raises growth when political freedoms are weak and lowers it when political freedoms are already well established.

capacity of a government. Economies can grow for decades without the government being able to extract more usable resources from them.[15]

Predictability and timeframe. In general, a reform strategy is observable. Indicators of economic growth, while imperfect, are well known and constantly reevaluated. Both governments and the private sector widely use GDP, productivity, investment levels, corruption indices, infant mortality rates, measures of trade and capital openness, and other measurements. Indeed, the lack of such information about a country usually indicates that it is not progressing economically: good data often correlate with economic transparency and an attractive business environment.

Reform takes decades to produce power. The British industrial "revolution" took some seventy years to reach full force and another half-century for its relative decline to become noticeable. So too with the United States, Germany, and Japan. Strong economies take decades to develop. Even several years of spectacular growth often can reverse, in essence a bubble rather than a long-term trend.

Degree of hegemon's concern. Because reform is both relatively predictable and takes decades, the initiation of a reform strategy may worry but seldom alarms the hegemon. The hegemon has years to probe the intentions of the rising state and to sway it in favor of the status quo. In addition, the very nature of the strategy—working with the international system in terms of trade and finance, promoting the rule of law, avoiding aggressive measures that might disrupt the growth environment, etc.—suggests that the rising power favors, rather than seeks to overturn, the status quo.

A key question when assessing reform is whether it is part of an overall strategy for power or simply desired as a good for society regardless of its international implications. This judgment is difficult, though discourse among leaders and in the public can provide some light onto the issue. In China today, reform is seen as a necessary precondition of power: until China has a strong economy and industrial base, it cannot achieve the power and influence it seeks.

[15]See Fareed Zakaria, *From Wealth to Power: The Unusual Origins of America's World Role*, Princeton, NJ: Princeton University Press, 1999.

For China, reform is thus a strategy.[16] Yet successful reform can lead even a benign power to change its strategic outlook and embrace conquest or other aggressive means of gaining influence.

THE REVOLUTION STRATEGY

Exploitation of a political or military revolution is a common but understudied source of state power. In contrast to reform, the exploitation of a revolutionary change in government or society can dramatically transform a state's capacity to extract resources, the country's ability to provide resources, or both. In addition, revolutions often lead to regimes with new foreign policy agendas and strong desires to overturn the status quo. Such transformations are often far more sudden—and far more difficult to anticipate—than more conventional power shifts.

Revolutions defy easy description. The term "revolution" has been used to describe political changes such as the Russian Revolution, military innovations such as the development of *blitzkrieg*, and social transformations such as industrialization and the spread of nationalism. For our purposes, a revolution is a change that results in a fundamental shift in government or alters the sources of national wealth and power. After a revolution, what "counts" for measuring power often changes, and a government's transformational capacity is often completely altered.

This section focuses on two types of revolutions—political and military—in assessing how revolutionary change can affect overall power.[17] The sources of revolution are numerous, complex, and always hotly debated. Humiliation in war, subjugation to a foreign power, financial crises, the emergence of new social elites, and a corrupt existing system all have motivated revolutionaries in the past. However, the true causes of almost every major revolution are still

---

[16]See Zalmay Khalilzad et al., *The United States and a Rising China,* Santa Monica, CA: RAND, 1999, and Michael D. Swaine and Ashley J. Tellis, *Interpreting China's Grand Strategy,* Santa Monica, CA: RAND, 2000.

[17]The line between reform and revolution often blurs. At times, social and economic developments can also be considered "revolutionary." As these are generally slow moving, they are assessed under "reform."

debated by historians. Almost all revolutions are highly contingent in their development and appear to follow few rules.

Characteristics of Political Revolutions

Political revolutions dramatically change the way a country is governed. A change from one regime to another, even of a different type, is not enough to constitute a political revolution. Rather, a political revolution produces a dramatic shift in the methods by which a country is governed and usually introduces an entire new class of governing elites and institutions. Under this definition, the French, the Russian, the Chinese nationalist and communist, the Cuban, and the Iranian revolutions are true political revolutions.

Revolutions can come from above or below. The French, the Russian, and the Iranian revolutions, among others, all involved outsiders overthrowing the entrenched order and building a new one in its place. Ataturk's Turkey and Meiji Japan, on the other hand, involved a small group of committed bureaucrats and leaders who implemented a "revolution from above."[18] These revolutionaries totally restructured society and government, but they did it from within the old system. Although the motivations and means for the revolutions from above vary considerably from those from below, both radically transform the social order.

The Nature of the Challenge

Revolutions and power changes. Political revolutions change transformational capacity but have little immediate effect on raw power inputs. Political revolutions by definition bring about a new government, which generally has different institutions that affect the state's ability to extract resources. Thus, the new regime often has an improved, or at least different, ability to extract resources. The Bolshevik regime, for example, proved itself able to force a rapid industrialization on Russia, and the French revolutionaries created a mass army: impossible changes under previous regimes. The resource

---

[18]See Ellen Kay Trimberger, *Revolution from Above: Military Bureaucrats and Development in Japan, Turkey, Egypt, and Peru,* New Brunswick, NJ: Transaction Books, 1978, for a description of this phenomenon.

base of these countries did not change, but the revolutionary governments were far better at exploiting resources.

State strength often grows for several reasons after a political revolution. First, weak states are more susceptible to revolutions; simply to survive and endure, a successor government must be stronger. Second, in the immediate aftermath, rivals mobilize social groups and try to exploit the power of existing resources. This revolutionary strife and competition tend to produce strong groups that are deeply rooted in society.[19] Third, revolutions often destroy entrenched social classes and interests, which in the past had impeded modernization, liberalization, or other types of change.[20]

Strengthened by political revolutions, the state is better able to implement social and economic reforms. Stronger states can implement reforms to increase the education levels, technological development, and other vital inputs to modern power. Thus, revolutionary change is often necessary to establish a leadership that will implement the reform strategy described above.

It is worth noting that revolutions often hinder rather than help economic growth. Various communist revolutions, the Iranian revolution, and other dramatic changes often led to stagnation and economies that had little capacity to compete on the global market. Revolutions often destroy productive classes. The instability they generate undermines the rule of law and the business and investment climate. Thus, while revolutions can be a source of power, commonly they are a source of decline.

Another common and dramatic result of the revolution is an increased capacity for war. The stronger state that emerges from the revolution is, of course, more able to extract resources and sustain popular will for a conflict. But the revolution can confer other advantages for war. The types of organization that helped the revolutionary leadership triumph over the old regime often translate well into international conflict. Guerrilla armies and intelligence services, for example, produce warriors and spies that can enable states to

---

[19]Theda Skocpol, "Social Revolutions and Mass Military Mobilization," *World Politics*, 40:2 (January 1988), p. 149.

[20]Trimberger, *Revolution from Above*, p. 3.

wage war better. Revolutionary regimes are generally able to exploit nationalism, enabling them to bring new elites together with older ones.[21] Revolutionary states also can wage far more costly wars, as populaces are often willing to sacrifice their lives and treasure to preserve the revolution.

Revolutionary change can lead to explosive growth and a dramatic increase in power. Every country in the world could be run more efficiently. Even countries with highly effective structures of governance have ample room for improvement that could lead to much higher economic growth. Nor are current structures, even in their most efficient forms, necessarily ideal to maximize power. Political innovation offers the potential for tremendous increases in economic growth and overall power. China has long had a strong central government, but its economy, dragged down by socialism, was too weak to provide the country with a high level of power. If China or other countries with tremendous human and natural resources could dramatically reform their economies, a tremendous growth in power might follow. Nor is economic transformation the only potential venue for revolutionary change. India, for example, has a relatively weak state due to the many fractures of Indian society. An India with a strong sense of national unity—and a far more efficient government and market—would be formidable indeed.[22] Such changes might go beyond limited reforms and dramatically increase these countries' power. As noted in the previous section on reform, flexibility is key to economic success: thus, revolutions today might allow countries to capitalize on future economic trends, even if the structures they establish appear ill suited for today's economy.

Predictability and timeframe. Predicting a revolution is quite difficult. Scholars have suggested a range of factors that produce revolution, including class struggle, foreign domination, and regime weakness, but no consistent patterns have emerged for what are complex,

---

[21]Skocpol, "Social Revolutions," pp. 149–150.

[22]The political revolution that may most dramatically change power today is the spread of liberal democracy. In most countries it has touched, it has increased economic efficiency. Of course, it has changed the transformational capacity of the state dramatically, allowing it to command greater loyalty from the citizenry, but it has restricted the state's freedom of action commensurately.

rare, and often unique events. Moreover, political revolutions can occur quickly, with no fixed path of development.

The change in state strength is another key measure of a revolution that is difficult to predict. For a state to exploit a revolution, it must have the capacity for systemic exploitation of the changes it has caused. Analysts should consider whether the new regime can harness nationalism to increase its power; whether the revolution's ideology is compatible with the factors that contribute to growth; whether the revolutionary regime is strong at home; and whether the regime can mobilize society. While intentions can change rapidly with a revolutionary regime, power buildup often takes more time. Revolutionary change often allows a country to grow much faster, tearing down obstacles to growth that hindered development. (Though, more commonly, the chaos of the revolution and its ideology often hinder development.) The key change is transformational, allowing the regime to do more with existing resources.

Revolutions can occur quickly. Although years of insurrection preceded the successful Chinese Communist takeover of power, in Russia, Meiji Japan, Kemalist Turkey, France, and Iran, revolutionary regimes took power without a long, drawn-out battle, though in several instances extended civil wars occurred after the revolution. In these latter cases, the regime's intentions, allies, and overall conduct changed almost overnight.

Degree of hegemon's concern. Although revolutions do not necessarily increase a state's power, the hegemon must be wary of the new regime. Particularly when powerful states undergo a revolution, the hegemon will watch carefully—previous commitments and peaceful behavior are no longer a reliable guide for future action. Revolutionary states are often highly aggressive and have an ideology that promotes conflict. In addition, revolutionary ideology often rejects the existing system, which the hegemon champions.[23] Some regimes can also generate more power by mobilizing the society and implementing economic changes, thus unsettling regional and global power balances.

---

[23]On revolutionary intentions, see Stephen M. Walt, *Revolution and War,* Ithaca, NY: Cornell University Press, 1996.

Characteristics of Military Revolutions

Dramatic political change is not the only revolutionary strategy. Countries can dramatically increase their power by exploiting a military revolution.

A military revolution typically rests on exploiting a technological breakthrough. Accurate, light-weight artillery, breach-loading rifles, the railroad, and improved fortifications are only a few examples of how technological breakthroughs dramatically changed the nature of warfare.

At times, however, the technology that leads to a "revolution in military affairs" (RMA) is not new, or the concept exploited is organizational or social. The German *blitzkrieg* exploited advances in tanks, aircraft, and radio, but it depended for success on doctrinal changes that had begun in 1917. These changes included the effective use of combined arms, small unit maneuver, deep penetration, and low-level commander initiative.[24]

Indeed, technology alone is not sufficient: the RMA must include changes in organization, doctrine, and strategy to exploit the benefits that new technology confers.[25] Andrew Krepinevich argues that technological change is only the first step. Development of military systems, innovation in military operations, and the adaptation of the organization to exploit these innovations must follow.[26]

Implementing an RMA often requires a more capable military and a more expensive one, but there are exceptions. New fortifications, new types of navies, air forces, and other revolutionary tools of war all required vast expenditures, many of which made it impossible for small states to survive financially in the face of military rivals. These

---

[24]Stephen Biddle, "The Past as Prologue: Assessing Theories of Future Warfare," *Security Studies*, 8:1 (Autumn 1998), pp. 46–47.

[25]Stephen Blank, "Preparing for the Next War: Reflections on the Revolution in Military Affairs," *Strategic Review*, 24:2 (Spring 1996), p. 17.

[26]Andrew Krepinevich, "From Cavalry to Computer: The Pattern of Military Revolution," *The National Interest*, 37 (Fall 1994), p. 30.

cost differences often led to huge differentials in military capabilities, with poorer and smaller states not only having fewer numbers of soldiers, but also less advanced militaries. Yet some RMAs, such as the musket, decreased the costs of fielding large armies.[27] These "cheaper" RMAs allowed more powers to access the latest military advances, leveling the field.

Cost is not the only, or even the most important, factor inhibiting the development of an RMA. Some militaries resist innovation. China, for example, discovered the gun first and had a metal-barreled cannon in the mid-13th century. But it rejected ship-borne artillery and never integrated the gun into its land forces effectively, making it vulnerable to Western domination centuries later.[28] Similarly, Turkish military forces in the late 17th century proved poor innovators, leading to steady losses to Western armies. Despite prodding from several sultans, the Turkish military remained conservative even in the face of repeated defeats.[29] For most of the interwar period, British politicians saw the British army as a colonial police force and thus discouraged it from developing the necessary forces and tactics for a fight on the continent.[30] All these states had the resources but neither the inclination nor the will to implement sweeping change. Table 2.2 summarizes some of the categories of military innovations.

What all of this shows is that a variety of factors, ranging from access to specific technology, willingness to pay the costs, as well as a set of historically specific circumstances all matter whether a given state can proceed with an RMA. Without any one of these, the RMA may not happen.

---

[27]Geoffrey Parker, *The Military Revolution: Military Innovation and the Rise of the West, 1500–1800,* New York: Cambridge University Press, 1996, pp. 12 and 17.

[28]Ibid., p. 83.

[29]Ibid., pp. 126–127.

[30]Williamson Murray, "Armored Warfare: The British, French, and German Experiences," in Williamson Murray and Allan R. Millett (eds.), *Military Innovation in the Interwar Period,* Cambridge: Cambridge University Press, 1996, p. 10.

Table 2.1

Selected Military Innovations

Technical	Tactical, Doctrinal, and Organizational	Macrosocial Innovations
English longbow	Mongol horse-archer tactics	Arming and training commoners ca. 1300
Machine guns	Mongol psychological warfare	Professionalization of armies and officer corps
Radio	Swiss pike square	Standardization of weapons
Railroad	Ship of the line tactics	Centralized taxation
Steam ship	Gustavus Adolphus' gunpowder tactics	Nation in arms
Internal combustion engine	Napoleon's General Staff system	Industrialization
Aircraft	Blitzkrieg	Freedom of information
Nuclear weapons	Strategic bombing	

SOURCE: Emily O. Goldman and Richard B. Andres, "Systemic Effects of Military Innovation and Diffusion," *Security Studies*, 8:4 (Summer 1999), pp. 94–97.

The Nature of the Threat

Power changes. Harnessing a military revolution can give a state's military a qualitative edge over its rivals, giving it an influence out of proportion to the rest of a state's power.[31] Thus, minor powers can quickly become major powers, while major powers can challenge the dominant power in the system despite having otherwise inferior power resources. States that were unable to adapt or exploit an RMA often were conquered or lost influence.

Successful exploitation of an RMA largely results in a transformative change in a state's power, allowing it to gain more military power from the same core inputs or population, resources, and so on. An RMA allows the military establishment to extract more power pro-

---

[31]For an argument that many so-called RMAs are in fact an evolution rather than a radical break, see Biddle, "The Past as Prologue." See also A. J. Bacevich, "Just War II: Morality and High-Technology," *The National Interest*, 45 (Fall 1996), pp. 37–47.

jection, combat strength, or other sources of military power through its revolutionary techniques. But an RMA can also have implications at the input level. Before the mechanization of warfare, for example, access to oil reserves was not an important power resource; but after oil-burning engines were placed in ships, trucks, tanks, and air-planes, it became vital. As the "chess pieces" that matter change, so too do the power resources that create or sustain these pieces.[32]

Predictability and timeframe. An RMA is often difficult to anticipate or recognize. Many revolutions are only clear in retrospect: only after they proved their mettle was their importance recognized.[33] Because revolutions depend on innovation and organizational change as well as technology, no single advance signals a revolution. By its very nature, an RMA involves using technologies, operational concepts, and organizations that have never been employed before: judging their effectiveness is difficult until they are tested on the battlefield. Indeed, history is littered with innovations that failed despite their theoretical promise.[34]

Analysts can, however, judge whether an RMA is being sought. The decision to pursue an RMA can happen quite quickly. A new leader-ship, a new security threat, or other factor that changes a state's mo-tivations can lead it to pursue an RMA. For analysts, this can involve macro judgments about whether a state has ambitious foreign policy objectives or faces a dangerous security environment, as well as more micro-intelligence on the doctrine and strategy of a state's security establishment. The organizational and doctrinal changes that rival militaries make are usually relatively open for intelligence analysis.

---

[32]This concept of an RMA ushering in new units (such as the armored division or the fighter wing) is taken from Eliot Cohen, "A Revolution in Warfare," *Foreign Affairs* 75:2 (March/April 1996), pp. 37–54.

[33]For a sobering, and amusing, look at mistaken expert predictions, see Christopher Cerf and Victor Navasky, *The Experts Speak*, New York: Villard, 1998.

[34]For an example, see Brian Bond and Williamson Murray, "British Armed Forces, 1918–1939," in Allan R. Millett and Williamson Murray (eds.), *Military Effectiveness, Volume II*, Boston: Unwin Hyman, 1988, pp. 112–113. Another frequently cited example of a misidentified revolution is the U.S. Army's move to a nuclear mission in the 1950s. See Andrew J. Bacevich, *The Pentomic Era: The U.S. Army Between Korea and Vietnam*, Washington, D.C.: National Defense University Press, 1986.

Moreover, the complexity and cost of warfare today probably make exploiting an RMA difficult for all but a few militaries. War is expensive: the Soviet Union declined in part because of its inability to sustain massive military spending. The budget for any one of the U.S. armed services exceeds that of the entire military budget for any other country. Even if a rival did develop an RMA, the United States would have the resources to emulate it, and probably surpass it, in short order. Of course, the conceptual ability to recognize an RMA and the administrative flexibility to adapt quickly to it are crucial in such a response.

The advantages to the state that first exploits an RMA often do not last long. Militaries learn, particularly defeated ones. Thus, they often incorporate the technologies and emulate the organization of their adversary.[35] Over time, the enemy with the most resources often exploits the RMA most thoroughly simply because it has more capacity.[36] In addition to learning, adversaries develop countermeasures.[37]

Despite these limits, even a temporary advantage may be enough to secure victory if otherwise evenly matched. By 1941, France might have adapted its doctrine to meet the needs of *blitzkrieg* warfare, but it was defeated too quickly to do so. Thus, even though an RMA's duration may be temporary, it is enough to change the military balance and affect the survival of states.

Degree of hegemon's concern. The advantages conferred by an RMA can help a state challenge the hegemonic power in a number of ways. In contrast to political revolutions, RMAs do not change a regime's motivations (in fact, new motivations may lead a regime to seek an RMA). Nevertheless, the uncertainty that surrounds the development and application of new technologies and concepts is likely to lead the hegemon to tread cautiously. Most obviously, a rising power

---

[35]Raymond E. Franck, Jr. and Gregory G. Hildebrandt, "Competitive Aspects of the Contemporary Military-Technical Revolution: Potential Military Rivals to the U.S.," *Defense Analysis*, 12:2 (August 1996), p. 245.

[36]Jeremy Shapiro, "Information and War," in Zalmay Khalilzad, John P. White, and Andrew W. Marshall, *Strategic Appraisal: The Changing Role of Information in Warfare*, Santa Monica, CA: RAND, MR-1016-AF, 1999, pp. 113–154.

[37]Biddle, "The Past as Prologue," p. 12.

that successfully harnesses an RMA can defeat the dominant power, despite the latter's overall superiority, and thus gain an advantage that may be impossible to erase. More frequently, the rising power can defeat a host of smaller and lesser powers, enabling it to conquer territory and draw additional power accordingly—as discussed below under "conquest."

THE ALLIANCE STRATEGY

Characteristics

One possible strategy for challenging the hegemon is for hostile powers to ally, using their combined resources to challenge the dominant power. Indeed, given the current resource disparity between the United States and possible challengers, alliance may be the only strategy available to potential competitors in the near future.

For states seeking to compete with the United States, alliances have three primary functions: aggregating power resources (the combination of power resources, primarily military, of the alliance members), enhancing power resources (use of an ally's knowledge and resources to increase a state's own ability to generate power), and denying the U.S. access to key strategic regions. Due to the frictions inherent in joint efforts, however, the realizable power potential of an alliance will generally be less than the sum of its parts. The effectiveness of a coalition's power aggregation will thus be influenced by the degree of its military and political integration and coordination.

A military alliance is an agreement between two or more states as to the conditions under which they will use military force. Such agreements are usually formal, with their conditions written and officially ratified by the parties involved. However, it is possible to have informal agreements functionally equate to a written alliance.[38] Thus a military alliance can range from a tacit understanding

---

[38]Jack Levy, "Alliance Formation and War Behavior: An Analysis of the Great Powers, 1495–1975," *Journal of Conflict Resolution,* 25:4 (December 1981), p. 587; Glenn H. Snyder, *Alliance Politics,* Ithaca, NY: Cornell University Press, 1997, p. 4; Stephen M. Walt, *The Origins of Alliances,* Ithaca, NY: Cornell University Press, 1987, p. 12. The U.S. security relationship with Israel is one example of an informal alliance.

between two or more states as to the conditions under which one will provide military assistance to the other(s), to a highly integrated organization such as NATO.

Although the classic alliance is defensive, the offensive alliance is the key type for the purposes of this study. Rather than provide security, the primary motivation for offensive alliances is to alter the existing international status quo.[39] The Nazi-Soviet Non-Aggression Treaty is an example of an offensive alliance because both states also wanted to redraw the map of Europe.[40]

Alliance tightness. The more cohesive the alliance, the more military power and strategic coordination it can generate. The power gains due to increasing alliance cohesion result from a reduction of the various "frictions" that reduce a coalition's military efficiency. Such friction can arise from disagreements over the basic objectives of the war at the strategic level, or over such minute details as incompatible tactical communications equipment. These frictions mean that a military coalition cannot be as effective as a similar-sized national force directed by a single command authority. Alliance tightness, by increasing the similarity between the coalition forces and a national army, tends to reduce frictions and thus make the alliance more militarily powerful.

A coalition of U.S. rivals will probably find it difficult to use increased alliance cohesion to narrow a power gap between them and the United States. The paucity of historical examples of tight alliances, particularly offensive ones, strongly suggests that such coalitions are difficult to form.

Several factors contribute to alliance tightness:

- Fear is probably the most important factor. States that believe they cannot defend their security interests will have a strong incentive to seek allies and to maximize the power of the alliance.

---

[39]Randall L. Schweller, "Bandwagoning for Profit: Bringing the Revisionist State Back In," *International Security*, 19:1 (Summer 1994), pp. 75, 79, 88–98; A.F.K. Organski, *World Politics*, New York: Alfred A. Knopf, 1958, pp. 330–333.

[40]Randall L. Schweller, "Tripolarity and the Second World War," *International Studies Quarterly*, 37:1 (March 1993), p. 76.

- Interest commonality is another important factor. The more that allied interests overlap, the less need there is to preserve autonomy to pursue interests outside of the alliance structure.

- The distribution of power in an alliance can also have an important effect. It will generally be easier for a tight alliance to form when it has a dominant member.[41] The preponderant power can either impose tightness upon alliance through coercion, much as the Soviet Union did on the Warsaw Pact, or facilitate tightness by bearing a larger share of the alliance costs or offering significant side payments. In addition, smaller powers will often be willing to trade autonomy for greater security.[42]

- The geographical or spatial distribution of the allies can also influence their ability to form cohesive alliances. The ally or allies directly adjacent or immediately vulnerable to the potential threat may have a greater interest in a tight alliance than their coalition partners who are less vulnerable. By avoiding a strong commitment, the second-line states can ensure that the front-line state bears the brunt of the peacetime alliance costs and that their own shares of the wartime costs are limited.[43]

- A shared ideology also contributes cohesion. NATO has always had a strong ideological agenda (democratization) that is evident in its founding document (the Washington Treaty), its main "visionary" documents (such as the Harmel Report), its actions (taking in new members on the basis of political and ideological, rather than strictly military, criteria), and its entire manner of functioning.[44]

---

[41]See Mancur Olson, Jr. and Richard Zeckhauser, "An Economic Theory of Alliances," *Review of Economics and Statistics*, 48:3 (August 1966), pp. 266–279, for a review of collective action and alliances.

[42]James Morrow, "Alliances and Asymmetry: An Alternative to the Capability Aggregation Model of Alliances," *American Journal of Political Science*, 35:4 (November 1991), pp. 913–916.

[43]Thomas J. Christensen, "Perceptions and Alliances in Europe, 1865–1940," *International Organization*, 51:1 (Winter 1997), pp. 67–68.

[44]NATO illustrates the daunting requirements of institutionalization needed for tight alliances. Because of the expectation—for much of NATO's lifetime—that the Soviet military threat would persist and the calculation that militarily the alliance faced unfavorable odds, the extent of military integration in NATO proceeded far, so as to offset the numerical disadvantages through gains in efficiency. At the level of inter-

- Finally, the hegemon's response is an important counterpressure to increased alliance tightness. In a system dominated by one power, states will often be loath to risk the loss of political, economic, and security benefits that can flow from a friendly relationship with that power. In addition, hegemonic powers often have the resources available to bribe or co-opt potential balancers into remaining relatively quiescent.

The Nature of the Threat

The power advantages of alliances. The single most important advantage that an alliance can provide is an immediate increase in usable power resources. The power provided, however, relies more on the alliance's tightness than on the simple amalgamation of its members' forces. The power provided is largely at the "input" level—increases in manpower, greater geographic range, technology sharing, and so on.

Most obviously, an alliance can increase the size of the members' military forces. It can also provide strategic benefits not directly related to an increase in power through aggregation. These benefits include the possibility of attaining a "virtual" global reach, reducing the number of potential opponents, and complicating a rival's strategic calculations and plans. Having a reliable ally in a region of strategic importance, one that is willing to provide bases in the area or will use its own forces to pursue the alliance's objectives, can provide a state with a substitute power-projection capability. States can thus use their allies to project power into regions that would otherwise be unreachable.

Alliances can also improve the basic components of national power available to a state. Through direct technology transfers from an ally, a state may be able to acquire the ability to produce and develop technologies that it would find too difficult, expensive, or time-

---

operability of the hardware used by the armed forces of members, there are now thousands of standardization agreements (STANAGs) that tried to make weapon systems of alliance members compatible and reduce the logistics footprint. NATO also developed extensive doctrine covering training and operations. These efforts took decades, required constant updating and evaluation, and yet still fall far short of interoperability.

consuming to develop on its own. Alliances can also help ensure the member states' access to such vital natural resources as food, energy, critical materials, and rare metals that either cannot be produced internally or could potentially be denied to them by others. An alliance can also improve a state's combat proficiency by exposing it to better doctrine, more experienced military personnel, and expanded training opportunities.

The power limits of alliances. Power accrued through alliances is not as reliable or efficient as power that is generated internally.[45] This weakness is apparent at the strategic level, with the possibility that an ally not only might not honor its commitments, but also put its own interests ahead of the collective good. In addition, differences in such factors as training, equipment, doctrine, and commitments mean that the end strength of an alliance is somewhat less than the sum of its parts. Furthermore, the various "frictions" that reduce alliance strength can be difficult to calculate. This difficulty increases the possibility that a state's foreign policy will be based upon erroneous calculations as to the relative strength of the alliance and thus result in costly mistakes.[46]

Because allies are not always reliable, it is necessary to discount the potential power gain achieved through alliance formation by a "loyalty coefficient." In the absence of a binding enforcement mechanism, a state can never be sure that its partners will honor their commitments.[47] Major powers generally aid their allies since they do not, as a rule, make alliance commitments lightly.[48] However, the main problem is not whether states will completely fail to honor their alliance commitments, but rather how they will choose to honor them. Even when states do honor their commitments, their support

---

[45]See James Morrow, "Arms Versus Allies: Trade-offs in the Search for Security," *International Organization,* 47:2 (Spring 1993)., pp. 207–234 .

[46]Kenneth Waltz, *Theory of International Politics,* Reading, MA: Addison-Wesley, 1979, p. 168.

[47]Glenn H. Snyder, "Alliances, Balance, and Stability," *International Organization,* 45:1 (Winter 1991), p. 132.

[48]Michael Altfeld finds that states nearly always honor their defense pacts when an ally is attacked. Indeed, with the exception of Italy in 1914, it is difficult to find a great power that failed to honor significant alliance commitments that it had made to another great power. Michael Altfeld, "The Decision to Ally: A Theory and Test," *The Western Political Quarterly,* 37:4 (December 1984), p. 526.

is often of dubious quality. It was cold comfort to the Poles in 1939 that France and Great Britain dutifully declared war on Germany but failed to go on the offensive because they believed that sacrificing Poland was necessary in order to win the war in the long run.

The problems of divergent interests and credibility of commitment will come into play most forcefully in alliances that are primarily offensive in nature.[49] The members of such a coalition rarely share more than a common obstacle to realizing their revisionist goals. They thus have a powerful incentive to limit the military resources they must divert from the pursuit of their own goals to support their ally. The strength of such alliances is further limited by the likelihood that once an ally achieves its goals, it will end or reduce its commitment, and by the vulnerability of such alliances to an opponent's strategy of divide and conquer.

Loss of autonomy is another cost of an alliance. States joining an alliance will have less freedom in defining and pursuing their own interests than those that do not. For instance, a state may need to tailor the structure and deployment of its military to take into account the military requirements of the alliance. Depending upon the nature of these requirements, a state could then find it difficult to use its military for non-alliance-related interests. In its most extreme manifestations, this loss of autonomy can result in a state being dragged into a war provoked by its ally.

Another power-related problem associated with alliance is that of free riding. This problem occurs when one state, having received a security guarantee from another, decides either to reduce the level of security that it provides for itself or to provide less than its "fair share." If free riding is a problem, the alliance does not increase the overall resources significantly.

Tight alliances also are often cumbersome in making decisions. All alliance members seek input into decisionmaking, which makes the process at best cumbersome and at worst intractable. A failure to consult with alliance members, however, risks the alliance's cohesion.

---

[49]Robert Jervis, "Cooperation Under the Security Dilemma," *World Politics*, 30:2 (January 1978), pp. 204–205.

Alliances can also negatively affect a state's external security. In essence, any state's attempt to improve its relative power position is likely to provoke a counterresponse from other states. Because an alliance is a highly visible form of power aggregation, it will be more likely to fuel such a response—a response that will increase as the alliance grows tighter and thus potentially more dangerous.[50] This potential security loss will be particularly great if the target of the alliance is the system's preponderant power. A state such as the United States has the ability for great reward or punishment. As a result, few states will be willing to risk its wrath unless they perceive that an alliance will confer significant benefits.

The disadvantages that come with alienating the hegemon will be more relevant to states that are seeking security. States that are willing to take risks to make favorable adjustments in the status quo will discount many of the above disadvantages and focus primarily on an alliance's relative ability to make these changes. The ability to form these offensive alliances thus rests upon how important the revisionist goals are to the states pursuing them and how willing the hegemon is to prevent their achievement.

Predictability. Determining whether an alliance will be formed, how close it will be, and the power that can be gained from it are difficult questions. Although alliances usually form in response to threat, they can also occur for a range of other reasons—particularly if the states in question are eager to change the status quo. In such cases, alliances can be forged (or, for that matter, abandoned) literally overnight. Twentieth-century examples, such as the Nazi-Soviet Pact, demonstrate why status quo regimes must worry that enemies (even ones hostile to each other) might join together to change the existing order. Once formed, it is difficult to predict how tight an alliance will be and the power it can produce. A host of conditions that produce or hinder tight alliances are discussed above, but measuring these in practice is often difficult.

Timeframe. Tighter alliances—ones that produce the most power— take time to build. This suggests that coordinated military operations are not likely to take place for many years, allowing the hegemon

---

[50]Snyder, *Alliance Politics,* p. 46.

considerable breathing space. Tighter agreements that involve the coordination of military forces or the synchronization of strategies will take longer to implement, particularly if they require the redeployment of forces or a change in military organization or size to meet the new obligations. Particularly tight alliances, such as NATO, can take decades to fully develop. Thus, the timeframe depends on the cohesion of the alliance: alliance members can coordinate their actions in the near term, but integrated operations take far longer.

Degree of hegemon's concern. Even though a tight alliance may take many years to build, the hegemon is likely to respond actively to an offensive alliance designed to change the status quo, for several reasons. First, the formation of an alliance suggests an obvious intent: the alliance members have, in essence, declared themselves dedicated to changing the status quo. Second, prudent hegemons are likely to overestimate the power of a hostile alliance, focusing on its potential while discounting the many factors that hinder tightness and overall coordination.

Being the hegemon, however, confers tremendous advantages when confronting an alliance: the hegemon can bully or buy potential allies to build its own power and undercut that of its rivals. Any power considering an alliance must assess how the United States will respond (and how important regional powers will respond). They may refrain from forming an alliance, or from taking steps to make a loose alliance tighter, in response to U.S. threats and inducements. The United States could even gain in terms of relative power if the new alliance provokes a counterbalancing coalition in its favor.

THE CONQUEST STRATEGY

Characteristics

A rising power can also try to increase its strength by conquering territory. The term "conquest" is used here to describe a whole range of forceful and intimidating behaviors leading to subjugation of a target country. These behaviors range from the use of (or threat to use) force to effect annexation or establishment of a "sphere of influence" and privileged access to the given state's resources, to an outright invasion and military occupation. Conquest has long been the most frequently traveled route to power. Persia, Rome, China, Spain, and other empires often began with a small city or region that steadily expanded, forcing outlying areas to knuckle under and become part of the empire. As territory grew, so too did power.

The value of conquest lies in the accumulation of resources.[51]   By bringing additional land under common rule, empires increased the manpower, natural resources, geographic advantages, and other sources of power of the overall state. The link between power and territory has continued to the modern era. Indeed, the entire focus of containment during the Cold War emphasized protecting leading industrial states to avoid their being conquered and/or turned into satellites and subsequent exploitation under Soviet rule.

Conquest typically requires large and capable military forces, or at least forces that are larger and more capable than those of the target and its allies. Occupation and assimilation of the conquered territory and people often require even larger forces as well as financial resources to sustain them.

The motivations for conquest range considerably. Regimes often want more territory for settlers, redress for a historic grievance, scarce resources, to secure markets, to use nationalism to bolster their standing at home, or a combination of these factors.

The Nature of the Challenge

Power advantages. In general, conquest changes a state's available inputs but does not strengthen its transformational capacity. The types of resources gained vary according to the nature of the conquest and actions of the conqueror. Rome gained more warriors, relying heavily on its Italian subjects to fight on behalf of the empire. Iraq's short-lived conquest of Kuwait offered the promise of almost 10 percent of the world's proven petroleum reserves. After World War II, the Soviets brought German scientists to the USSR, using their expertise to develop the Soviet missile and space programs. Resources can also be geostrategic. Britain's conquest of Gibraltar from Spain enabled it to control access to the Mediterranean even

---

[51]The cumulativity of resources is assumed by many leading political scientists. See Waltz, *Theory of International Politics*, p. 172.

though Gibraltar, by itself, offered little in terms of natural or human resources.

Many of the natural resources gained from conquest may have limited value in peacetime, particularly if the world's economic order is relatively open, but tremendous importance should war occur. For example, oil extracted from the newly conquered hinterland may be more expensive than oil received in trade. But if trade is not an option—blockade and sanctions are the rule, not the exception, in war—then the extra reserves may be invaluable.

Although natural resources can transfer almost entirely, this is not so for industrial resources. Peter Liberman estimates that Nazi Germany extracted between 19 and 44 percent of the prewar national incomes from the west European states it conquered; immediately after World War II, the Soviets transferred 23 percent of East Germany's GNP.[52] This suggests that power can increase considerably through conquest, but also that a high "discount level" must be applied.

Not all states can extract resources from industrial societies. A high degree of coercion is needed. Both the Nazis and the Soviets prevented wide-scale unrest in the modern industrialized states they conquered through brutality and terror. In contrast, democratic states are often poor conquerors, as they face more (though hardly overwhelming) constraints in killing, repressing, and otherwise keeping the subject population down. Thus, they typically spend more resources keeping order than they gain from the occupied state.[53]

The more the power resources of the conquered territory lie in knowledge and human capital, the less susceptible they are to conquest. Physical resources and industrial stock can be transferred, as can a few key workers who can be bullied and bribed. Many skilled

---

[52]Peter Liberman, *Does Conquest Pay? The Exploitation of Occupied Industrial Societies*, Princeton, NJ: Princeton University Press, 1996. This figure is all the more impressive, given that governments only extract roughly 50 percent from their own populations (the rest being necessary to feed, clothe, shelter, and otherwise care for them).

[53]Liberman, *Does Conquest Pay?*

workers will emigrate—and those with the most skills are the best able to depart.[54]

Empire, of course, carries a price. In what Liberman has labeled the "quagmire" theory, many scholars argue that empires—particularly modern empires—require more resources to control than can be gained from them.[55] Particularly in the age of modern nationalism, conquered countries often resist attempts to exploit their resources. Latter-day Alexanders thus often "overstretch" themselves and spend more resources policing their holdings than they derive from the conquest itself.[56]

The costs of empire are also geopolitical. Conquering powers are likely to provoke a balancing coalition against them. Both the accumulation of power by a neighbor and the obvious threat that the neighbor has demonstrated through the act of conquest leads nearby states to form coalitions against the emerging power. Thus Czarist Russia and Germany found themselves "surrounded" by hostile states concerned about their growing power.

Predictability. A necessary condition for successful conquest is sufficient military power. Thus, standard measures well known to military analysts on the size and quality of military forces are essential for judging whether conquest is a feasible strategy. For the purposes of anticipating a peer competitor, however, it is equally important to assess the costs and benefits of the conquest itself. Analysts must assess the likely level of resistance to the conqueror, the ability of a state to pacify conquered territory, and the costs of doing so. The type of resources gained requires particular scrutiny to judge whether they will significantly increase a conqueror's power.

---

[54]Stephen G. Brooks, "The Globalization of Production and the Changing Benefits of Conquest," *Journal of Conflict Resolution,* 43:5 (October 1999), pp. 646–670; see also Stephen Van Evera, "Primed for Peace," *International Security,* 15:3 (Winter 1990/91), pp. 14–15.

[55]See Liberman, *Does Conquest Pay?* p. 9, for a discussion.

[56]For arguments on overstretch, see Paul M. Kennedy, *The Rise and Fall of the Great Powers: Economic Change and Military Conflict from 1500 to 2000,* New York: Random House, 1987, and Robert Gilpin, *War and Change in World Politics,* Cambridge and New York: Cambridge University Press, 1981.

Timeframe. Although a conquest can occur in a matter of days, in general it takes years or more to assimilate the resources—particularly when the captured territory is large and requires an elaborate coercion mechanism. Thus, while conquest demonstrates a hostile intent and states must respond to it if they fear being conquered in turn, the fact of a conquest does not necessarily tilt the balance of power in favor of the conqueror. Through successful conquest, a state can immediately gain favorable geography and access to an existing military and industrial infrastructure. Integrating this infrastructure more fully, to say nothing of making the conquered people supportive of their new master, is far harder.

Degree of hegemon's concern. A conquest strategy almost always challenges the hegemon. Most obviously, it suggests hostile motivations on the part of the rising power. By using force, the rising power demonstrates its willingness to flout the rules of the game (the latest edition, at least) to achieve its ambitions. In addition, successful conquest can increase a country's power, adding people, resources, and territory that can be exploited in a confrontation with the hegemon. Conquest also challenges the hegemon's role as defender of the status quo, raising the question of whether the hegemon is, indeed, strong enough to defend the current system. Fortunately for the hegemon, conquests often alarm potential allies, making them more likely to work with the hegemon against the rising power.[57]

Does Conquest Still Pay?

Historically, conquest may be the most important source of power, but its relevance has declined dramatically in the last fifty years. Conquest is a rocky path to power and has both political and economic costs.[58] Several costs make it difficult to initiate and sustain a conquest:

---

[57]There are instances where the hegemon will support, or at least not oppose, a conquest. Britain, for example, supported Japan's extension of influence in Asia before World War I, believing that this would help Britain because Great Britain and Japan were allies. But these instances are rare. Particularly in today's world, the U.S.-supported order emphasizes the illegitimacy of conquest, making the hegemon's support for a conquest particularly unlikely.

[58]This summary of arguments is drawn from Brooks, "The Globalization of Production," p. 648.

- The spread of powerful weapons, particularly nuclear weapons, that can devastate even "victorious" powers;
- Frequent strong resistance to going to war on the part of many publics, particularly democracies;
- The need to sacrifice additional lives and money to pacify the conquered territory;
- Losses of trade from interdependent economies.

Aggressive states are also likely to provoke counterbalancing coalitions. Germany's aggressive rhetoric and ambitions in the run-up to World War I gradually drove Britain to ally with France and Russia. This pattern is as close to a general rule as international relations theory offers: status quo states balance against hostile threats. If a country sought to build up its forces and otherwise increase its offensive power, its neighbors—the probable first victims of any expansion—usually would build up against it. Thus, the United States could work against an aggressive China, Russia, or other powers simply by aiding the forces of their strong and willing neighbors.[59]

The benefits of conquest have fallen in recent years even farther than the costs have increased. Transformative capacity has grown in importance for a state's overall power, while in the past overall resources played a greater role. The shift to knowledge-based economies has transformed the nature of wealth, and with it the benefits of conquest. The repression necessary for successful pacification is not always compatible with the free flow of information. Information-age industries may wilt in such an environment. Conquerors usually centralize decisionmaking to ensure control, further hindering innovation. The economic assets also are often mobile. In the past, land and capital stocks could be seized and wealth thus gained; information assets, however, follow skilled employees, many of whom often emigrate in response to war. Without these employees, advanced machinery will be of limited use at best. A decline in risk capital is likely to follow a war and the resultant change in regime, further decreasing innovation. Of the production

---

[59]William C. Wohlforth, "The Stability of a Unipolar World," *International Security,* 24:1 (Summer 1999), pp. 28–31.

assets that remain, they are often only a small part of an overall system rather than the entire value-added chain. Finally, an open trade and investment system allows states to gain many of the benefits of war without paying the political and economic costs.[60]

This combination of higher costs of going to war and fewer benefits has made war and conquest less practicable and therefore less desirable. As such, we contend that conquest is a far less useful path to becoming a peer competitor today than in the past, and that it carries more risks. But the argument that conquest is now a less valuable strategy does not mean that war with conquest aims will not occur in the future or that it has ceased to be an option for certain types of proto-peers. Depending on the specific opportunity structure, a strategy of conquest may not have ceased to be an option for some states as a path to power aggregation. Nevertheless, wars over secession, irredentism, and other internally motivated strife are still more likely than wars of conquest, and such wars affect the overall power balance relatively little.[61]

---

[60]Brooks, "The Globalization of Production," pp. 656–665.

[61]For a persuasive argument along these lines, see Michael Mandelbaum, "Is Major War Obsolete?" *Survival*, 40:4 (Winter 1998–1999), pp. 20–38. For an influential earlier work arguing the obsolescence of major war, see John Mueller, *Retreat from Doomsday: The Obsolescence of Major War*, New York: Basic Books, 1989.

Chapter Three

THE ROLE OF THE HEGEMON

A proto-peer does not exist in a vacuum. Its choice of a strategy, the extent of its dissatisfaction with the status quo, and its potential to pursue a path that leads to competition and rivalry with the hegemon are influenced profoundly by the power differential between itself and the hegemon, the net rate of change in that power, and the actions of other players. Among the latter, hegemon actions are particularly important, since that is the state that the proto-peer may challenge and the one it uses to measure its own progress. Indeed, a dynamic process of interaction takes place between the proto-peer and the hegemon that shapes the degree of success that the proto-peer achieves in developing national power.

The preceding chapter presented, by way of analytical constructs, the proto-peer's set of long-term strategies for power aggregation. This chapter, after outlining the assumptions that underpin the hegemon's role in the international state system, examines the rationale and the choice of strategies (also analytical constructs) available to the hegemon for dealing with a proto-peer, most centrally in its ability to affect the proto-peer's aggregation of power.

THE HIERARCHY IN THE INTERNATIONAL STATE SYSTEM

Distinctions between states on the basis of their power act as an organizing principle within the international state system. In this sense, the international state system has a hierarchy, with the most powerful state at the top and the less powerful states at lower points, with their specific position depending on their power levels.[1]   The hegemon, or the state at the apex, establishes the "rules" of international relations and upholds the status quo structure governing relations between states.[2]   The "rules" established by the hegemon per-

---

[1]We accept the core assumptions of the realist paradigm: states are unitary actors operating in conditions of a lack of a sovereign power, relations within the international system are inherently conflictual in that states hold different preferences about the distribution of scarce resources, and outcomes of interstate bargaining over resources reflect the threats and incentives that, in turn, are based on the existing power structure. These core assumptions are widely shared among scholars of international relations. The assumption of rationality is not an essential one. Although we accept the view that states attempt to act in a purposive fashion, it is the underlying context—the international system—that socializes states into certain behavioral patterns. Within the realist paradigm, the power transition theory is most relevant to the problem of anticipating the rise of a peer competitor, as it deals specifically with the circumstances under which a challenge to the hegemon might take place and the path such a challenge might follow. The power transition theory focuses on a dyadic interaction, in opposition to the "balance of power" theory, which focuses on the systemic structure. Contrary to what some proponents of each theory advocate, we do not see the two theories as contradictory; they simply aim to explain different questions. Though we use insights from the power transition theory, we do so selectively. We do not subscribe to the idea of inevitability of conflict, nor do we accept the strictly economic formulation of national power that is common among the power transition theorists. For a recent review of the power transition literature, see Jonathan M. DiCicco and Jack S. Levy, "Power Shifts and Problem Shifts: The Evolution of the Power Transition Research Program," *Journal of Conflict Resolution*, 43:6 (December 1999), pp. 675–704. For the seminal works in the power transition literature, see A.F.K. Organski, *World Politics*, New York: Alfred A. Knopf, 1958; A.F.K. Organski and Jacek Kugler, *The War Ledger*, Chicago: University of Chicago Press, 1980; and Jacek Kugler and Douglas Lemke (eds.), *Parity and War: Evaluations and Extensions of "The War Ledger,"* Ann Arbor, MI: University of Michigan Press, 1996. For a prospective look at the power transition theory as it applies to potential conflicts in the 21st century, see Ronald L. Tammen, Jacek Kugler, Douglas Lemke, Allan C. Stam III, Mark Abdollahian, Carole Alsharabati, Brian Efird, and A.F.K. Organski, *Power Transitions: Strategies for the 21st Century*, New York and London: Chatham House Publishers, 2000. For a rebuttal of the proposition that the balance of power and power transition theories are contradictory, see Randall L. Schweller and William C. Wohlforth, "Power Test: Evaluating Realism in Response to the End of the Cold War," *Security Studies*, 9:3 (Spring 2000), pp. 60–107.

[2]It is a basic assumption here that the state will remain a fundamental building block of human global relations for the foreseeable future, even as its roles and functions change in accordance with technological advances and the accompanying social changes. The phenomenon has evolved enormously over the past few centuries, from the dynastic state of overlapping jurisdictions to the contemporary demarcated state, and it will no doubt continue to evolve and adopt to the new circumstances of greater interdependence and communication. The growth—over the course of the 20th century—of international organizations and the emergence of norms that delegitimize the use of force have provided new conflict-resolution mechanisms for states and, arguably, have placed some constraints on the use of force. However, such long-term

tain to the functioning and structure of international political and economic interactions. For example, after World War II, with the United States ascending to a role of the hegemon in the international state system, it played a leading role in establishing such institutions as the United Nations, the Bretton Woods system, the International Monetary Fund, and a host of others.[3] These institutions either were new or replaced ones with a similar role (such as the United Nations replacing the League of Nations), and the United States has dominated their functioning. Similarly, and fitting its hegemon's role of upholding the rules, the United States has played a consistent role as the ultimate arbiter and mediator in international conflicts since the end of World War II.[4]

Within the hierarchy of power in the international state system, the main distinction is between the states that are satisfied with the rules and those that are not. By definition, since the hegemon sets up and then upholds the rules, the hegemon is satisfied. But many other states perceive the rules as detrimental or at least not optimal in terms of their interests and, to a varying extent, are dissatisfied. Dissatisfaction may stem from any number of reasons, ranging from being excluded from setting up the rules to dependence on domestic political interests that see themselves penalized by the rules.

---

trends have not altered the fundamental state-centric power basis of international politics, even though they may have curtailed the incidence of armed interstate conflict. As long as power remains the currency of politics among states, international conflict and militarized disputes will be a potential outgrowth of power relations. For some critiques of the "end of the state" literature, see Linda Weiss, *The Myth of the Powerless State*, Ithaca, NY: Cornell University Press, 1998; Stephen D. Krasner, *Sovereignty: Organized Hypocrisy*, Princeton, NJ: Princeton University Press, 1999; and Guenther G. Schulze and Heinrich W. Ursprung, "Globalisation of the Economy and the Nation State," *The World Economy*, 22:3 (May 1999), pp. 295–352. For the impact of norms on state behavior, see Andrew P. Cortell and James W. Davis, Jr., "How Do International Institutions Matter? The Domestic Impact of International Rules and Norms," *International Studies Quarterly*, 40:4 (December 1996), pp. 451–478.

[3]The case of the United States is unique in modern history in that, in the first half of the 20th century, it was among the most powerful, if not the single most powerful, country in the world but, until the end of World War II, was not the hegemon and did not use the full extent of its power to advance its position in the power hierarchy of states. An explanation of U.S. behavior within the conciliate strategy of the existing hegemon is offered below.

[4]This is shown empirically in Jacob Bercovitch and Gerald Schneider, "Who Mediates? The Political Economy of International Conflict Management," *Journal of Peace Research*, 37:2 (2000), pp. 145–165.

Satisfied states have a stake in the preservation of the rules, since they gain from it. Dissatisfied states have less of a stake in the system or oppose it. Either way, dissatisfied states want to change the rules to structure the system in a way that gives them greater advantages. The combination of (1) the extent of power disparity between the hegemon and the dissatisfied state and (2) the level of a state's dissatisfaction with the rules of the international system mainly determines whether a dissatisfied state will compete within those rules.

An attempt to change the basic rules of the international system without the hegemon's permission (i.e., an effort that is noncooperative vis-à-vis the hegemon and threatens the hegemon's position) contains the potential to evolve into military conflict. Therefore, any state contemplating such a challenge must consider it carefully. If the challenge evolves into a crisis in which the challenger backs down, that challenger will lose power, having been shown unable to follow through with a threat. Moreover, the hegemon is likely to remain wary of future challenges and adjust its policy toward such a dissatisfied state accordingly. If the challenge escalates to a military conflict, then the challenger has to consider the possibility of catastrophic defeat.

The hegemon has little leeway, since failing to respond to a challenger that openly violates the rules amounts to an admission that it cannot enforce the rules, leading to a loss of relative power between it and the challenger. Not surprisingly, empirical studies show that challenges to the hegemon generally occur when the challenger has about as much power as the hegemon, with power parity calculated in a dyadic fashion and defined as the challenging state having at least 80 percent of the hegemon's power.[5] At parity, the challenger may believe that it stands to make a net gain even if a military conflict ensues. In short, at parity, the danger of a military conflict between the principals is the greatest, since both think they can win.

---

[5]Stuart A. Bremer, "Dangerous Dyads: Conditions Affecting the Likelihood of Interstate War: 1816–1965," *Journal of Conflict Resolution*, 36:2 (1992), pp. 309–341; William Brian Moul, "Balances of Power and the Escalation to War of Serious Disputes among the European Great Powers, 1815–1939: Some Evidence," *American Journal of Political Science*, 32:2 (May 1988), pp. 241–275. Though the above studies do not deal with the patterns of conflict in the last thirty years, there is no reason to believe that such a basic characteristic of international conflict has changed.

Whether the risk of war is worth it to the challenger depends on how dissatisfied it is with the rules and its calculation of the potential net gain from changing them. In other words, the challenger needs to calculate an expected gain before challenging the hegemon. Power parity enhances the chances that such a calculation will come out positively, but ultimately it is the regime-specific calculation of potential gains and losses that leads to a conflict.

The Hegemon's Problem

The most fundamental question that the hegemon faces is how to remain one. Power distribution within the international state system is always changing, as the power of some states grows at faster (or slower) rates relative to the hegemon. Under such conditions, the hegemon must constantly calculate and recalculate the power ratios and make projections, with the ultimate policy concern being how to preserve its dominant position at the least cost. The question is most difficult in conditions of parity or near parity, but it remains a major policy challenge even under conditions of huge power disparities. This is so because the hegemon relies on the submission to its rules by the other main actors to sustain its hegemonic role. Using coercion to uphold the rules, however, can alienate as well as intimidate. Thus, the hegemon must steer carefully, employing positive incentives toward those states that are willing to behave in accordance with the rules, even adjusting them at times to deflect potential challenges, and using force only toward those states clearly unwilling to abide by the rules.[6]

---

[6]The behavior described here is based on the concept of general deterrence, defined as an adversarial relationship between two states in which the leadership in one state would consider resorting to force to change the status quo but is deterred from doing so because the leadership in the other state, knowing that the opponent is willing to use force, maintains force of its own and makes it clear that it will retaliate against the opponent's use of force that is contrary to its own interests. If a hegemon were to rely on outright coercion to sustain its role within the international state system, such a stance would be bound to be short-lived, since it would raise the levels of dissatisfaction among the other major actors in the state system. Even in conditions of huge power disparity between the hegemon and other main actors in the state system, the hegemon's position would be untenable if all the other major actors were to unite against it. On general deterrence, see Patrick Morgan, *Deterrence: A Conceptual Analysis*, 2nd ed., Beverly Hills: Sage, 1983, pp. 42–43.

The hegemon must pursue different strategies toward the various proto-peers and prospective competitors, depending on the assessment of the other main actors' propensity to comply "voluntarily" with the rules. The main difference among the strategies lies in the extent of conflict imposed within the strategy, with conflict referring to the exacting of additional costs from the proto-peer that it would not otherwise incur.[7] Examples of conflict imposition include anything from trade tariffs that offset a comparative advantage a proto-peer may have, to incitement of internal unrest, to favoring a neighboring rival, all the way to a military strategy that forces the proto-peer to build up its military forces and siphon off investment funds. The common thread among them is that the hegemon's actions force the proto-peer to divert attention, money, and effort in ways the hegemon sees as inimical to the proto-peer's optimal power growth. Thus, conflict imposition is the primary means of reducing a proto-peer's power growth rate. The mere threat of a hegemon imposing greater degree of conflict onto a proto-peer has a deterrent effect and greatly influences the proto-peer's behavior and its choice of a strategy for power growth. The greater the hegemon's preponderance of power and the greater the power differential between it and the proto-peer, the more likely the proto-peer is to tread carefully and consider how the hegemon perceives its behavior, because the consequences of incurring the hegemon's wrath are greater.[8]

Absence of conflict imposition and inclusion of positive incentives are the other side of the coin in the hegemon's strategy. A lack of conflict imposition in the hegemon's strategy is the norm and should

---

[7]The idea of conflict imposition as a tool of state policy against a perceived rival builds on Richardson's seminal work on arms races: Lewis F. Richardson, *Arms and Insecurity*, Pittsburgh: Boxwood, 1960. Kadera proposed the concept of conflictual behavior as a policy tool and provided a formal proof of the link between a state's power level and its ability to direct conflict against perceived rivals. The concept of conflict imposition, as used here, builds on Kadera's work. Though similar to "cost imposition," the term "conflict imposition" is more nuanced in that it refers to a growing set of conflictual relations (which entail costs), though not necessarily militarized relations. Kelly M. Kadera, "The Power-Conflict Story: A Synopsis," *Conflict Management and Peace Science*, 17:2 (Fall 1999), pp. 149–174.

[8]The value of conflict imposition as a policy tool in preventing certain actions and the importance of greater capabilities for this deterrent to be effective has been demonstrated by looking at U.S. use of force since the 1950s; see James Meernik, "Force and Influence in International Crises," *Conflict Management and Peace Science*, 17:1 (1999), pp. 103–131.

be expected by the other main actors in the international state system, since the hegemon rewards the states that adhere to the rules with cooperation. However, it is the perception (by other states) of the hegemon's ability to impose conflict that leads others, sometimes grudgingly, to adhere to the rules.

Although the hegemon is in a strong position, it faces a continuous and difficult calculation of the proper mix of conflict-imposing policies in its strategy toward a proto-peer. If the hegemon reacts with more force and conflict than are warranted, then it may strengthen that proto-peer's determination to become a peer and a competitor. On the other hand, if the strategy is too conciliatory in that it contains less conflict imposition than the proto-peer's behavior warrants, then the hegemon risks hastening the emergence of a peer and potentially a competitor.

The hegemon's decision on the extent of conflict imposition toward a proto-peer stems from a threat assessment that has two main elements. First, the hegemon assesses its own future vulnerability to a specific proto-peer, based on projections of its own and the proto-peer's growth. Second, the hegemon also assesses the specific proto-peer's revisionist tendencies, based on projections of future power growth estimates. The first assesses other actors' ability to achieve parity, while the second assesses other actors' likelihood of becoming competitors.

Because of the profound nature of a potential challenge a peer may pose and the enormous costs that competition entails, the hegemon must be prudent and consider all possible actors that may emerge as peers within a generation (20–25 years) and their likelihood of challenging the hegemon's rules. For identified proto-peers, estimates even beyond the quarter-century mark are prudent.

The assessment of both power growth and revisionist potential has two essential characteristics. First, it is primarily dyadic, focusing on the two central actors' projected power levels. Likely allies are only considered secondarily, since the proto-peer's ability to gain major allies depends on dyadically calculated chances of success. The assessment of revisionist potential is also dyadic. At issue is the specific proto-peer's level of dissatisfaction with the system (and thus, the hegemon) and consequent determination to pursue a path toward parity that may lead to tradeoffs in the search for allies.

Second, the assessment is made at both the regional and global levels. In other words, the hegemon assesses the proto-peer's projected power level in the region where the proto-peer is located as well as in the international state system. In cases of power preponderance and projections of no global peer emerging within a generation, a proto-peer may still be present at the regional level. Since the hegemon has global commitments, it cannot commit all its power and resources to one region. However, a proto-peer can concentrate almost all of its resources in its own region. The assessment and projections need to take this disparity into account. Similarly, the hegemon needs to assess the proto-peer's level of dissatisfaction with a regional status quo as well as with the larger rules of the international state system. In conditions where peers and proto-peers likely to be competitors are clearly present, the hegemon's assessment is even more complicated, because it needs to take into account the attraction of the proto-peer to other dissatisfied actors and how that may impinge on the global position of the hegemon.

All the calculations and assessments made above are fraught with deep uncertainty because of the long time frame involved. Extrapolations on the basis of existing trends have little use beyond the short term, since nonlinear evolution is more the rule than the exception when it comes to long-term projections. However, forecasting nonlinear change with any kind of confidence remains virtually impossible, because no technique has yet been developed that would predict a nonlinear occurrence before the actual event.[9] Since the correct strategy can be discerned only retrospectively, the hegemon faces the decision on how much conflict imposition it should include in its strategy toward a proto-peer, knowing that the range of error is bound to be substantial and to grow larger as the time frame lengthens. Moreover, the assessment is subject to error along both the power growth and revisionist axes.

---

[9]Charles F. Doran, "Why Forecasts Fail: The Limits and Potential of Forecasting in International Relations and Economics," *International Studies Review*, 1:2 (1999), pp. 11–41.

The Hegemon's Strategies

Just as the proto-peer has a limited number of power-growth strategies, the hegemon too has a limited set of strategies for dealing with a proto-peer. With the primary point of reference for distinguishing among the hegemon's strategies being the extent of conflict imposition they contain, there are four main strategies realistically available. They range from emphasis on cooperation and avoidance of conflict imposition, to a hedging strategy with a predominance of cooperative aspects, to a hedging strategy emphasizing conflict-imposition elements, to a highly competitive strategy that emphasizes conflict imposition. We refer to these four strategies as conciliate, co-opt, constrain, and compete.

The strategies are analytical constructs, identifiable by the extent of conflict imposition within them and, at a deeper level, by the whole range of calculations and a resulting threat assessment that lead to the adoption of a specific strategy. The relationship between the hegemon's threat perception and the extent of conflict imposition in its strategy toward a proto-peer is directly proportional, though the costs to the hegemon of a specific strategy imposition may not be proportional to its effect on the proto-peer. Figure 3.1 provides a notional representation of the relationship. The 20, 40, 60, and 80 percent marks represent the median points of the extent of conflict imposition in each strategy, though there is a range within each and an overlapping area between them.

Theoretically, the range of strategies could be extended further, to include extreme cases of (1) total absence of conflict imposition and (2) total conflict imposition. The first amounts to a surrender by a hegemon to a proto-peer, whereas the second means a preventive war. Although both are theoretically possible, neither is plausible because of the fundamental uncertainty about the evolution of the proto-peer (as outlined above) and the potentially enormous costs entailed by a mistaken assessment leading to the adoption of such a strategy. The conciliate and compete strategies are the realistic end points on strategy choices for the hegemon (and, in any event, the upper portion of the compete strategy comes close to a preventive war). We describe each of the strategies in detail below.

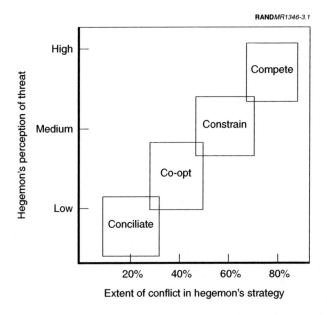

Figure 3.1—Hegemon's Strategies

THE CONCILIATE STRATEGY

The conciliate strategy has the goal of increasing common interests between the proto-peer and the hegemon, thus giving the proto-peer incentives not to challenge the rules established by the hegemon as well as a greater stake in the system. The strategy has a minimal amount of conflict-imposition elements. The hegemon's goal is to limit friction with the proto-peer, and the strategy is predicated on allowing the proto-peer's rapid growth. The hegemon's desired result is a peer that is a potential ally rather than a competitor.

To pursue this strategy, the hegemon must assess the threat of the proto-peer as low, based on a calculation that the proto-peer has low revisionist tendencies and that such tendencies, even with a leap to parity, will remain low. In fact, by choosing the strategy that is low in conflict imposition, the hegemon is betting on the preservation of the main elements of the rules even if the proto-peer were to over- take the hegemon. There is also the expectation that if a proto-peer were to overtake the hegemon, the transition to a new hegemon would take place without armed conflict since the two states have largely similar interests. No reigning hegemon ever desires a power transition, for it entails the loss of the most privileged status and the decisive voice in establishing the rules. Every hegemon will be reluctant to give up its position. No matter how much common interests may link the old and new hegemon, even a friendly power transition introduces some uncertainty about the old hegemon's rules and the potential for the old and new hegemons to retain the same level of common interests in the future. But it is a rational strategy under certain circumstances.

The conciliate strategy may apply when a proto-peer's power is projected to grow at a high rate (and bound to overtake the hegemon within a generation), it does so within the rules, and the hegemon does not assess such a proto-peer as having major revisionist potential. Although the prospect of being replaced by another state is never pleasant, the old hegemon expects that it will fade slowly because of common interests with the new hegemon and knows that it will retain the resources that otherwise would have been squandered on competition. Moreover, after such a friendly transition, the old hegemon would retain a powerful role in shaping the further evolution of the new one. In other words, the competition would not have been worth the costs, for two reasons. First, such competition would only have encouraged revisionist tendencies in the proto-peer (creating the potential for substantial changes to the rules and leading the proto-peer to penalize the old hegemon if it won), leading to a situation that could be much worse than the one absent the competition. Second, the goal of such competition, which would probably take enormous resources to win, would not be all that different from an end goal of a friendly power transition.

The higher the expected rate of power growth relative to the hegemon, the more conciliatory the strategy is likely to be. The higher relative growth rate and expected power transition simply make the cost calculations of potential competition with such a proto-peer even less worthwhile. Conceivably, assuming a meteoric rise of a proto-peer and that all the conditions necessary for the adoption of the conciliate strategy are in place, the conflict-imposition content would decline to virtually nil.

When it has preponderant power, a hegemon is likely to be strict and cautious in interpreting a proto-peer's revisionist aspirations. Thus, proto-peers that exhibit a low level of revisionist tendencies might, rather than being treated with a conciliate strategy, be subjected to one with a higher conflict-imposition content. This occurs because the hegemon is used to having its way, leading it to overestimate the gravity of otherwise minor revisionist tendencies.

In the presence of several revisionist regional peers and proto-peers, the calculations that may lead a hegemon to adopt a conciliate strategy may be relaxed and lead to the strategy being adopted toward states that have either (1) moderately revisionist tendencies and high rates of power growth or (2) no revisionist tendencies and moderate or low rates of power growth. The crucial element here is the hegemon's assessment of the set of peers and proto-peers. In the first instance, if facing highly revisionist peers or proto-peers, the hegemon will need to pick the "least revisionist" one because it needs allies to engage in competition with, and fend off the challenge from, the more fundamentally dissatisfied proto-peers or peers. In the second instance, if facing fast-growing revisionist peers and proto-peers, the hegemon may choose to encourage the faster growth of a proto-peer whose rate of power aggregation is relatively slow but whose interests parallel the hegemon's. In both cases, the hegemon's calculations stem from a need to strengthen its own position when challenges loom. The choice of the course of action depends on the specific preferences of the hegemon and the overall threat assessment.

The British policy toward the United States beginning in the mid-1890s and the early 20th century provides an example of the conciliate strategy. Faced with a United States that was gaining power rapidly, confronted simultaneously with competition from France and Russia (later replaced by Germany), and realizing the vulnerability of British holdings in the western hemisphere (Canada) to the United States, Britain concluded that its interests would not be threatened by allowing the United States to assert regional hegemony over the western hemisphere and that such a move would gain it a potential ally against continental proto-peers and competitors. Thus, in a multiactor situation, the British made a calculated choice to avoid conflict with the United States and nurture it as a potential ally, a decision that, over several decades, led to a friendly power transition and retained for Britain many benefits of its earlier hegemony. Even today, the "special relationship" between the United States and the United Kingdom reflects the earlier policy choice. A contemporary example of the conciliate strategy might be the U.S. policy toward the European Union, as the EU has similar interests in upholding existing rules.

THE CO-OPT STRATEGY

The co-opt strategy is a hedging strategy designed to lower the potential for the proto-peer to compete with the hegemon. The strategy has a fair amount of conflict-imposition elements and the hegemon does not shy away from disputes with the proto-peer, though cooperative aspects form the majority of the hegemon's policies. This is a predominantly "carrots" hedging strategy, wherein the hegemon remains cautious about allowing a rapid rise of the proto-peer and uses the interim period to strengthen the proto-peer's tendencies in favor of the existing rules while avoiding overt conflict. The hegemon's desired result is to allow the rise of the proto-peer but with a sustained change in its behavior.

For this strategy to be pursued, the hegemon must assess the specific proto-peer as a moderate threat, based on a calculation that it has some revisionist tendencies but also that these tendencies could change in response to threats and blandishments. The expectation is that by the time the proto-peer attains parity with the hegemon, it will subscribe to most of the rules. In other words, by choosing this strategy, the hegemon is betting that the proto-peer's revisionist tendencies are not fundamental.

However, there is a cautionary note in the hegemon's assessment, in that a rapid rise of the proto-peer along its current path would be detrimental to the hegemon. In the hegemon's assessment, the proto-peer needs further behavioral adjustment. The hegemon realizes that this hedging strategy eventually may shift to a new strategy either upward (higher conflict imposition) or downward (lower conflict imposition) and that this strategy represents a temporary phase (though "temporary" may still mean a decade or more). If the proto-peer seen as warranting a co-opt strategy were to continue accruing power faster than the hegemon without moderating its revisionist tendencies, then the hegemon's assessment of the threat would grow and lead at least to a higher level of conflict imposition within the co-opt strategy or to a more punitive hedging strategy (the constrain option). On the other hand, if such a proto-peer were to moderate its revisionist inclinations and show greater acceptance of the rules, then the hegemon's assessment of the threat would decrease and lead to a lower level of conflict imposition within the co-opt strategy. If the proto-peer continued to accrue power at a fast rate and the hegemon were convinced that it no longer retained any revisionist tendencies because the co-opt strategy had worked, it might shift to a conciliate strategy.

A co-opt strategy may apply when a proto-peer's power is projected to grow at a high rate (and is bound to overtake the hegemon within a generation), and it either does not follow some of the rules or is assessed as likely to alter them substantively as it becomes more powerful. The revisionist potential of such a proto-peer cannot be regarded by the hegemon as fundamental, since it would then pursue a more punitive strategy. The revisionist tendencies must be pronounced and sufficiently threatening so that the hegemon is willing to expend resources, draw clear lines, and risk disputes with the proto-peer as part of its attempt to shape its evolution. In other words, the hegemon makes clear the limits of permissible behavior for such a proto-peer and is willing to raise its level of conflict imposition if they are exceeded. Although the strategy remains optimistic about shaping the long-term evolution of the proto-peer, the punitive consequences of straying from the envisioned path should be clear to all. Ultimately, the hegemon's calculation is that domestic interests that have a stake in upholding the rules will grow in importance in the proto-peer, while those with revisionist tendencies will lose out in a relative sense.

As for the range of conflict imposition within the co-opt strategy, the primary determinants of its higher levels are the combination of the projected rate of relative power growth and the extent of revisionist tendencies. When both are on the high end of the spectrum (while still fitting within the co-opt scale), then the co-opt strategy is likely to have a high content of conflict imposition, bordering on the constrain strategy. When the two are related inversely to each other, that is, either a moderate rate of power growth and more substantial revisionist tendencies or a high rate of power growth and less pronounced revisionist tendencies, then the strategy is likely to have a medium level of conflict imposition. The rationale stems from the less immediate threat assessment and longer time for the co-opt strategy to work in the first case above, to a lower assessment of overall threat and an emphasis on nurturing a fast-growing proto-peer in the second. When both are low, then conflict imposition is likely to be on the lower end of the strategy, bordering on the conciliate strategy.

When a hegemon has preponderant power, it tends to exaggerate threats and choose strategies that involve more conflict imposition than a proto-peer's capabilities might warrant. A proto-peer's revisionist aspirations that would, under conditions of a fundamental threat in a multiactor situation, be considered of low significance and amenable to a conciliate strategy, might be seen as more threatening and lead to a co-opt strategy. With several revisionist regional peers and proto-peers, whether a hegemon adopts a co-opt strategy depends greatly on the identification of the greatest or the most immediate threat and the assessment of other actors from that point of reference. If the proto-peer poses a clear and fundamental threat, the hegemon's scale of what are moderate revisionist tendencies may shift appreciably toward the more forgiving side and include proto-peers that otherwise would fit into the category of having more fundamental revisionist tendencies.

The decision on the direction of the shift vis-à-vis specific proto-peers depends on how long it would take the proto-peer to pose a more fundamental threat. With short-term threat, the hegemon decision to adopt a co-opt policy toward less-deserving proto-peers would focus more on a proto-peer growing in power rapidly. With longer-term threat, the hegemon would be more likely to adopt a co-opt policy toward a less-deserving proto-peer on the basis of its lower revisionist tendencies. In both cases, the hegemon's calculations stem from an evaluation of the time frame available to strengthen its own position in the face of a looming challenge. Beyond the above, the choice of the course of action may also be subject to additional specific preferences of the hegemon.

British policy toward Germany in the early 1890s provides an example of the co-opt strategy. The passing of Bismarck made Britain cautious about German intentions and led it to adopt a co-opt strategy. But as long as Germany remained outwardly muted in exhibiting revisionist tendencies toward the rules upheld by Britain, the British did not see a rapid rise of German power as problematic. Only with the rise of a more assertive German policy that directly challenged Britain (build-up of a navy and colonial ambitions) did the hedging strategy escalate toward more punitive elements and direct competition. A contemporary example of the co-opt strategy might be the U.S. policy toward China, based on goals of increasing the Chinese stake in the existing rules but also drawing clear lines on any use of force.

THE CONSTRAIN STRATEGY

The constrain strategy, too, is a hedging one, but it is designed to display the hegemon's ability to punish the proto-peer for flouting the existing rules. Most of the strategy's elements consist of conflict imposition, and the hegemon accepts a high level of disputes with the proto-peer. Yet cooperative elements still play a substantial role, and the hegemon hopes to prevent a militarized competition with the proto-peer. However, this is a predominantly "sticks" hedging strategy, whereby the hegemon is pessimistic about the chances of the proto-peer not turning into a competitor and uses the interim period to delay the proto-peer's leap to peer status and strengthen its antirevisionist tendencies in the meantime. The hegemon wants to slow the rate of power growth and effect a sustained change in the proto-peer's aspirations and behavior.

For this strategy to be pursued, the hegemon must assess the threat of a specific proto-peer as high, based on a calculation that the proto-peer has strong revisionist tendencies and that they cannot be altered easily. The hegemon's strategy focuses on constraining the proto-peer, so that, finding its power aggregation rate decreased over a prolonged period because of hegemon actions, it will shed some revisionist aspirations (because they will seem increasingly distant or unachievable) and reconcile itself to working within the hegemon's rules. The strategy entails mostly negatives because the hegemon wants to throw up as many obstacles as possible to the proto-peer's power aggregation, since it sees the leap to peer status as leading to a full challenge. In other words, by choosing this strategy, the hegemon is betting that the proto-peer potentially represents a fundamental threat and therefore wants to halt or at least slow its power growth. Because of the proto-peer's strong revisionist tendencies, positive incentives are not a wise choice for the hegemon, because they will only quicken the proto-peer's growth and emergence as a full-blown competitor. Positive incentives retain a role in that areas of common interests remain, and the hegemon is responsive to signs of moderation in the proto-peer's behavior. However, the dominant aspect of the constrain strategy is the hegemon's attempt to use conflict imposition to slow the pace of the emerging threat, decrease the proto-peer's revisionist tendencies, and buy time.

The hegemon realizes that this hedging strategy may eventually shift to an even more conflictual one, though it retains hopes that the negative incentives may work. Thus, if the proto-peer continues to accrue power faster than the hegemon and does so without moderating its revisionist tendencies (i.e., the constrain strategy fails), then the hegemon's assessment of the threat would grow and lead at least to a higher level of conflict imposition within the constrain strategy and perhaps even outright conflict (the compete strategy). On the other hand, if the strategy shows signs of eliciting the desired response, then the hegemon would decrease its assessment of the threat and, to encourage the positive behavior, employ less conflict imposition within the constrain strategy or shift to a lower conflict imposition strategy (co-opt). Either way, this is a hedging strategy, and it represents a temporary phase (though "temporary" may still mean a decade or more).

The constrain strategy may apply when a proto-peer aggregates power at a high rate (and is projected to overtake the hegemon within a generation) but follows the rules only loosely, and the hegemon assesses this proto-peer as having even less stake in the system as it becomes more powerful. The hegemon still sees a possibility that a sustained and punitive lesson may change the proto-peer's behavior, but, in the hegemon's assessment, its fundamental revisionist tendencies put it on a clear trajectory to becoming a major threat. As such, the hegemon is willing to expend resources and risk crises with the proto-peer as part of its punitive strategy. To the hegemon, the proto-peer must be shown the limits, or it will evolve into an even more powerful foe.

As for the range of conflict imposition within the constrain strategy, the combination of the proto-peer's projected rate of power growth and extent of its revisionist tendencies primarily determines the higher levels. When both are on the high end of the spectrum, then the constrain strategy is likely to have a high content of conflict imposition, bordering on the full-blown competition that characterizes the compete strategy. When the two are inversely related, that is, either a moderate rate of power growth and fundamental revisionist tendencies or a high rate of power growth and strong but not firmly entrenched revisionist tendencies, then the strategy is likely to have a medium level of conflict imposition. The rationale stems from the lower immediate threat assessment and longer time for the constrain strategy to work in the first case, to a lower assessment of overall threat and a greater possibility for positive incentives to have an effect. When both are low, then the conflict-imposition aspects are likely to be on the lower end of the strategy, bordering on the co-opt strategy.

In conditions of power preponderance, the hegemon is likely to have a propensity to view revisionist aspirations more cautiously; proto-peers that would, under conditions of a fundamental threat in a multiactor situation, be considered as amenable to a co-opt strategy might be assessed as warranting a constrain strategy instead. The probable low costs of conflict imposition to the hegemon may act as incentives to push the hegemon into adopting more punitive strategies than necessary, but the overall need for efficiency in the hegemon's actions will moderate such incentives. With several revisionist regional peers and proto-peers, the calculations that may lead a hegemon to adopt a constrain strategy depend greatly on the identification of the greatest or the most immediate threat and the assessment of other actors from that point of reference. When a hegemon is already engaged in a rivalry, a proto-peer that might otherwise be assessed as having fundamental revisionist tendencies may in fact be treated much more leniently, as in a lower end of conflict imposition within the constrain strategy. Such a proto-peer would have to be assessed by the hegemon as "less threatening" and the policy would be adopted only as the "less bad" choice. Specific preferences and contextual factors also would affect the hegemon's decision.

The British policy toward Russia in the 1890s and into the early 20th century (until 1905) provides an example of the constrain strategy. Russian challenges to British colonial possessions, its alliance with France, and the potential for its power to grow rapidly because of industrialization made it Britain's primary opponent. Only Russia's much lower overall power level led Britain to choose a constrain rather than compete strategy, in which the British focused on blockading further Russian inroads. There is no contemporary example of the constrain strategy, although, depending on China's potential further evolution, a U.S. shift to a constrain strategy toward China is plausible.

THE COMPETE STRATEGY

The compete strategy attempts to decrease the proto-peer's power relative to the hegemon by imposing conflict to punish the proto-peer. The strategy is highly conflictual. The hegemon's goal is to curtail the further growth of the proto-peer's power, and the strategy rests upon the hegemon's willingness to risk repeated militarized crises to effect change in the proto-peer. The hegemon already views the proto-peer as a competitor and wants to keep it from becoming a peer.

To pursue this strategy, the hegemon must assess the threat posed by a specific proto-peer as high, based on a calculation that the proto-peer has fundamental revisionist tendencies that are unlikely to be moderated by measures short of threat of force. By choosing a strategy high in conflict imposition, the hegemon is betting that the proto-peer represents a fundamental challenge to the rules and is willing to risk war to prevent it. The hegemon's assessment is that if the proto-peer were to overtake it, then the hegemon's current form of existence would be threatened. In other words, the hegemon expects a national calamity if it were to be overtaken by the proto-peer. The fundamental difference in interests leaves little room for positive incentives, and the hegemon expects that armed conflict would accompany any power transition. Rather than trying to channel the proto-peer's evolution into a more hegemon-friendly pathway, the hegemon emphasizes punishing the proto-peer and preventing any relative power. Given the assessment that the proto-peer has fundamental revisionist tendencies, the hegemon has little hope that less conflictual strategies might moderate the proto-peer's views. Moreover, the decision to embark on a compete strategy has long-term consequences. Once adopted, it is likely that domestic interests that have a stake in the competition will make it difficult to de-escalate.

The compete strategy may apply when a proto-peer aggregates power at a high rate (and is projected to overtake the hegemon within a generation), and it does so by flouting the established rules. The hegemon assesses such a proto-peer as not only having little stake in the system but also as fundamentally opposed to it, and the hegemon sees that opposition as likely to grow with the proto-peer's power. Reconciliation is impossible, and the hegemon calculates that the proto-peer must be stopped before it becomes even more powerful. Since the hegemon sees no alternative to sustained punishment as a way to deal with the challenge, it is willing to embark on what may be a long-term rivalry, expend massive resources, and risk crises. The hegemon is betting that the threat is so fundamental and the consequences of a power transition so calamitous that a costly rivalry is preferable.

As for the range of conflict imposition within the compete strategy, the higher the expected rate of relative power growth, the more conflictual the strategy is likely to be. The higher relative growth rate and, consequently, an expected earlier time frame for a power transition add urgency to the hegemon's actions and justify higher risk and costs. Since fundamental revisionist aspirations by the proto-peer are a given, any differentiation within the revisionist tendencies may affect the nuances of the hegemon's strategy but is not likely to modify greatly the extent of conflict imposition. Conceivably, given a proto-peer in a meteoric rise when all the conditions necessary for the adoption of the compete strategy are in place, conflict imposition would constitute almost all the actions of the hegemon.

Two issues regarding the compete strategy arise when the hegemon has preponderant power. First, a proto-peer that has such fundamental revisionist tendencies is less likely to appear because of the dominant role of the hegemon and its ability to isolate such a proto-peer at an early stage. Open flouting of the rules when the hegemon wields an enormous power advantage is not a rational way to aggregate power. Even dissatisfied proto-peers are likely to mute their revisionist tendencies, and they are bound to have some stake in the existing system. Second, the hegemon is likely to have a propensity to view revisionist aspirations with caution, thus tending to overestimate the level of threat the proto-peer poses. Eventually, over-estimation of the threat and adoption of a highly conflictual hedging strategy might lead to further escalation and adoption of the compete strategy.

With several revisionist regional peers and proto-peers present, the state posing the most fundamental threat soonest is going to be the target of the hegemon's compete strategy (assuming it meets the criterion of having fundamental revisionist tendencies). That state then would provide the hegemon with a frame of reference for judging other actors. Conceivably, if two states have fundamental revisionist aspirations, the hegemon might adopt a compete strategy toward one and a hedging strategy (either constrain or co-opt) toward the other. Thus, when a hegemon is already engaged in a rivalry, a proto-peer that might otherwise be assessed as having fundamental revisionist tendencies may in fact be treated much more leniently. Of course, if the hegemon were to emerge victorious over the main proto-peer, it would most likely reassess its policy toward what were previously assessed "less threatening" states.

The U.S. policy toward the USSR between the late 1940s and late 1980s provides an example of the compete strategy (with the most conflictual period in the 1950s and 1960s). The United States assessed the Soviet challenge as fundamental in that imposition of Soviet rules on the international system would have meant, at a minimum, a very different United States, both internally as well as in terms of U.S. relations with other countries. There is no contemporary example of the compete strategy, and such a shift seems implausible in the short term, although, in the long term, a U.S. shift toward such a strategy is plausible.

THE EFFECT OF POWER PREPONDERANCE

The hegemon's relative power within the international state system is a crucial variable underpinning the logic for adopting the strategies outlined above. A preponderance of power favors lasting hegemony, while a system of multiple actors with the hegemon being "first among equals" rather than in a class by itself make continued hegemony much more tenuous. There are simply more ways for proto-peers or existing peers to evolve as competitors when multiple actors are present. Conversely, the greater the gap in relative power, the less likely a proto-peer will be to choose an aggressive strategy, since it does not want to risk a confrontation that forces it to back down or suffer defeat (with all the consequences that implies).

Moreover, power preponderance is self-reinforcing in that it allows the hegemon to use less costly (meaning less conflict-imposition content) strategies toward proto-peers. Power preponderance provides the hegemon a safety margin. Internally centered power growth strategies by the proto-peer, even if highly successful, are bound to take many years, if not decades, to achieve parity with the hegemon. In that time, the hegemon can assess carefully the type of a challenge that may be in the making and, if necessary, build coalitions or affect the growth of the proto-peer accordingly. In addition, the potential to use the full spectrum of strategies toward a proto-peer, available because a challenge is not immediate, enables the hegemon's shaping policy to work, causing potentially competitive proto-peers to abandon or scale back revisionist tendencies. The greater the power preponderance, the greater the likelihood that the system of incentives and disincentives established by the hegemon will channel the proto-peer's evolution in line with the hegemon's intent.

The potential problem the hegemon faces when it has preponderant power that offsets partially the self-perpetuating characteristics is its own tendency to overestimate threats and potential challenges and adopt strategies that are unnecessarily conflictual. As long as the difference in power levels between the hegemon and a proto-peer remains the same or increases (in favor of the hegemon), this problem is absent. But when a proto-peer shows a faster rate of power growth than the hegemon, and the hegemon calculates that it could achieve parity in the foreseeable future, then the hegemon will see its position threatened and, even if the proto-peer is an ally, is likely to be suspicious. Thus, somewhat paradoxically, in conditions of power preponderance there is a stronger tendency for the hegemon to be wary of any major actor than there is with multiple actors and existing peers and proto-peers.[10] The costs of high-conflict-

---

[10]Prospect theory, with its premise that a decisionmaker will accept risks to avoid losses but will refuse to take risks to make similar gains, offers a link between overly cautious behavior and potentially conflict-generating behavior. Accepting the premise of prospect theory, it could be argued that the same would apply to the proto-

imposition strategies add up and weaken the hegemon in a relative sense, making it susceptible to other proto-peers. In addition, the hegemon faces the risk that its overestimation of the challenge from proto-peers may, in the aggregate, subtly shift the rules of the international state system that it upholds. For example, greater reliance on conflictual strategies may threaten other actors, leading to a coalition against the hegemon. Failing a shift in the rules toward a system upheld more by direct rather than implied power and sanctions, the more likely it is that a regional peer will challenge the status quo. In other words, a proto-peer with some revisionist tendencies is likely to attempt to alter regional hierarchy first. Because of its global responsibilities, the hegemon will be able to concentrate only a portion of its power at the regional level, whereas the regional proto-peer is likely to be able to concentrate almost all of its power there. In such circumstances and depending on the behavior of the other actors and their level of dissatisfaction with the rules, the proto-peer may force the hegemon to back down or accept an unfavorable compromise. Such an outcome has tremendous consequences for the hegemon's standing, since it shows that its power is less than others may have calculated.

PRINCIPAL RIVALRIES

Even when the hegemon tries to prevent the emergence of a peer by using highly conflictual strategies, a peer may emerge anyway. Alternatively, an exogenous shock might turn a benign and cooperative peer into a competitor. A transformation of an existing competitor into a peer, or the metamorphosis of an ally peer into a competi-

---

peer, making it similarly cautious. However, the consequences of the prospect theory may not apply in the same fashion to the proto-peer and the hegemon. For example, if the proto-peer perceives the risk of losing its relative power status, then it might adopt an extremely risky behavior to deal with the hegemon. The case of Japanese behavior in 1941 is a case in point. Although prospect theory is in direct challenge to rational choice approaches, empirical tests have shown its robustness in a variety of applications. See Paul A. Kowert and Margaret G. Hermann, "Who Takes Risks? Daring and Caution in Foreign Policy Making," *Journal of Conflict Resolution*, 41:5 (October 1997), pp. 611–637; Rose McDermott, *Risk-Taking in International Politics: Prospect Theory in American Foreign Policy*, Ann Arbor, MI: University of Michigan Press, 1998; and Kurt Weyland, "Risk Taking in Latin American Economic Restructuring: Lessons from Prospect Theory," *International Studies Quarterly*, 40:2 (June 1996), pp. 185–208.

tor, does not necessarily mean armed conflict with the hegemon. Though a war between such a peer competitor and the hegemon is certainly possible and the relationship may have numerous crises, the enormous costs of such a conflict and the potential catastrophic result that the loser would suffer dampen the prospects of such a war. Instead, a contentious rivalry may ensue.

A rivalry is a long-standing and competitive relationship between two states or two states and their allies. To meet the definition of a rivalry, a competition must have the following elements: the same set of adversaries, a perception of threat and hostility toward each other, and a temporal dimension that reflects the impact of previous interactions and shapes expectations of future interactions.[11] Rivalries usually come into being through an exogenous shock, such as civil wars, major interstate wars, or territorial changes. The common thread among the various shocks is a dramatic change in the distribution of power in the international state system.[12] While such sudden events trigger the rivalry, typically there has to have been an evolutionary decrease in the power difference between the proto-rivals. That evolutionary change may be linear in its slow drift into ever-greater competition, which generates further and greater conflicts that may eventually evolve into a rivalry.[13] In such cases, history matters and can condition each party toward a more escalatory and hostile response.[14] A large body of empirical data suggests that rivalries account for most of the world's conflicts and confrontations, and they are relatively more prone to escalation and war

---

[11]Paul F. Diehl (ed.), *The Dynamics of Enduring Rivalries,* Urbana: University of Illinois Press, 1998.

[12]Gary Goertz and Paul F. Diehl, "The Initiation and Termination of Enduring Rivalries: The Impact of Political Shocks," *American Journal of Political Science,* 39:1 (February 1995), pp. 30–52.

[13]Paul R. Hensel, "An Evolutionary Approach to the Study of Interstate Rivalry," *Conflict Management and Peace Science,* 17:2 (Fall 1999), pp. 175–206.

[14]Thomas Gautschi, "History Effects in Social Dilemma Situations," *Rationality and Society,* 12:2 (May 2000), pp. 131–162. A psychological explanation of this pattern is based on the decisionmakers' use of established behavioral templates in interpreting others' actions. Valerie M. Hudson, "Cultural Expectations of One's Own and Other Nations' Foreign Policy Action Templates," *Political Psychology,* 20:4 (December 1999), pp. 767–801.

than are confrontations between states not engaged in a rivalry.[15] Moreover, within rivalries, relations tend to become more conflictual over time, because once a rivalry is in place, it has self-perpetuating internal dynamics and becomes entrenched in domestic politics on both sides, making it increasingly difficult to break the cycle of competition and conflict.[16]

A rivalry between principal states, as between a hegemon and its main peer competitor, is the central axis of international relations in any given era. Although the rivalry may include disputes over resources or territory, such a "principal rivalry" is most of all about the power status of the competitors and their ability to establish rules. In other words, it is about the relative position of the two competitors in the hierarchy of the international state system, either in a specific region or on a global scale.[17]

Principal rivalries fall into two categories: global and regional-global.[18] Global rivalries pertain to competition for leadership at the apex of the international state system; they involve competition between a hegemon and a competitor that is at near parity with the hegemon and aspires to hegemony. Global-regional rivalries concern competition between a regional leader and the global leader; they involve a regional peer competing with the global hegemon to establish regional primacy. Regional primacy can then serve as a stepping stone to a global challenge. There is a premise here that a proto-peer's gaining of a regional leadership role is more power additive than power draining. Though this may not be necessarily true in practice, a prudent hegemon cannot take the chance that a proto-peer that is also a regional leader will use the new role inefficiently. Thus, the prudent hegemon will look with alarm upon any

---

[15]Russell J. Leng, "When Will They Ever Learn: Coercive Bargaining in Recurrent Crises," *Journal of Conflict Resolution*, 27:3 (September 1983), pp. 379–419.

[16]This is a widely supported finding. Paul K. Huth, "Enduring Rivalries and Territorial Disputes, 1950–1990," *Conflict Management and Peace Science*, 15:1 (1996), pp. 7–41.

[17]William R. Thompson, "Principal Rivalries," *Journal of Conflict Resolution*, 39:2 (June 1995), pp. 195–223.

[18]Thompson has suggested a distinction into three main types: regional, global, and regional-global. The categories suggested here are similar, though not the same as Thompson's categories. Regional rivalry falls outside the scope of our peer competitor work.

proto-peer aspiring to regional leadership in a fashion unsanctioned by the hegemon. Global rivalries arise when the hegemon plays the dominant role but at least one other actor is near parity with it. In other words, global rivalries do not arise when the hegemon is the preponderant, unless some exogenous shock rapidly transforms the international power hierarchy. On the other hand, global-regional rivalries can arise under conditions of power preponderance as well as power parity.

Principal rivalries usually last for decades and generations, since they pit states that are the most powerful and roughly comparable in power against each other. Because they are powerful, the states involved can draw on massive resources to fuel the rivalry. In an overall sense, principal rivalries are enormously expensive, since they entail war-like expenditures for decades. Global and global-regional rivalries differ somewhat in their propensity for war. On the basis of limited historical data, global rivalries tend to be relatively pacific in that open warfare between the two rivals is not a given, and war is often waged by their proxies and on the periphery of their areas of control. Eventually, one side wins but not necessarily as a result of a war between the two principals. Internal collapse or downgrading of power of one of the principals, due to exhaustion, and either a power transition to a new hegemon or a strengthening of the old hegemon's position, has been the primary way of ending a global principal rivalry.[19] In this sense, the outcome of the U.S.-Soviet rivalry is typical. Global-regional rivalries are more war-prone, if the limited historical data provide any indication of a larger pattern. The rise of a European regional leader has led to a militarized competition in almost every case during the past three centuries.

The high presence of war in global-regional rivalries is an anomaly to the logic of the evolution to war of principal rivals. The relative absence of war between principals in a global rivalry makes sense, since the two states are near parity and neither is eager to launch a war directly on the other because of the reasonable chance that it will lose. Thus, even though the conditions are in place for a war, it takes some miscalculation or propensity for risk on one side to bring about

---

[19]Thompson, "Principal Rivalries," p. 211.

a war between the principals. Consequently, the global principal rivalry is characterized by attrition.

The same logic applies to global-regional rivalry, the only difference being that parity is calculated at the regional level. That also explains the incidence of direct armed conflict between principals. The regional challenger's calculation of the hegemon's ability and willingness to engage in war in the challenger's region is subject to a serious error, namely, the different perspectives of the challenger and the hegemon. The challenger may see an incremental step on the path to a greater regional role as unlikely to provoke an armed response from the hegemon because the stakes in play are limited and important only at the subregional level. However, the hegemon's view is on the evolutionary trend of the regional challenger, its tendency not to abide by the rules, and its potential to become a regional hegemon that can then mount a global challenge. After a certain point, incremental changes within a region amount to a trend that the hegemon must curtail to avoid a greater challenge down the road. The end result of the different perceptions is a rivalry and, potentially, armed conflict.[20]

Whether or not the rivalry leads to armed conflict, the drawing of the United States into a principal rivalry is something that the intelligence community must anticipate at the earliest possible time, so as to alert the national decisionmakers and allow them to take appropriate steps either to head off the rivalry or prepare for it. Thinking about the emergence of a peer competitor boils down to the following point: under current conditions of U.S. power predominance in the world, the most important task is the early warning of an emerging principal rivalry. Unfortunately, identifying an evolving principal rivalry before it starts is impossible with any certainty. One problem is that the origins of the demand for positional goods—status—in the international state system are murky and difficult to translate into operational terms.[21] Moreover, some proto-peers may have a deep

---

[20]Kim and Morrow provide a formal proof of how risk-proneness and different evaluations of the meaning of a subregional conflict may lead to a major war. Woosang Kim and James D. Morrow, "When Do Power Shifts Lead to War?" *American Journal of Political Science*, 36:4 (November 1992), pp. 896–922.

[21]Higher status means higher costs, by way of increased expenditures on defense (to uphold that status) and greater likelihood of using the military, yet the benefits of such

interest in allying with the hegemon as a way of gaining power and status.[22] However, keeping in mind that the hegemon's threat perception and the proto-peer's pace of power growth provide a key axis of the relationship and determine the choices of strategy for each, a matrix of the proto-peer strategies for power aggregation and the hegemon's shaping strategies provides a starting point for observations on the evolution of principal rivalries. The logic behind the evolution to a rivalry can be illustrated by the use of simple game theory, which we describe in detail in the next chapter.

---

a status are not easily identifiable. Hans Kammler, "Not for Security Only: The Demand for International Status and Defence Expenditure: An Introduction," *Defence and Peace Economics*, 8:1 (1997), pp. 1–18.

[22]Structural theories posit little choice for states and decisionmakers, treating a drift toward confrontation among the major powers as a given and as inevitable. Such a line of thought, dismissing choice and regime latitude in deciding to engage in competition, is overly deterministic, and empirical evidence does not support it. The realist paradigm is helpful in that it provides a way of thinking about the behavior of states and how they advance their interests, but the prioritization of interests is internally determined. John A. Vasquez, *The War Puzzle*, Cambridge: Cambridge University Press, 1993; Bruce Bueno de Mesquita and David Lalman, *War and Reason: Domestic and International Imperatives*, New Haven, CT: Yale University Press, 1992; and Patrick James, "Structural Realism and the Causes of War," *Mershon International Studies Review*, 39 (1995), pp. 181–208.

Chapter Four

MODELING THE PEER-HEGEMON RELATIONSHIP

If the adoption of more competitive strategies by both the proto-peer and the hegemon heralds an emerging principal rivalry, how could the precursors of such a rivalry be identified? In other words, how can one identify a potential principal rivalry between a hegemon and an emerging peer when the proto-peer is still pursuing an internally focused power aggregation strategy and the hegemon is following a primarily cooperative strategy? This question has no single answer, but it is possible to identify some determinants of the evolution toward a higher (more competitive) mix of strategies. Modeling the interaction of strategies allows for a clearer look at how one actor's behavior affects the other actor and the overall direction of the relations between the two. Modeling the interaction can help identify trends toward a principal rivalry.[1]

The modeling approach rests on the relationship between two things. The first is the rate of increase of a proto-peer's power, with national power defined in a holistic fashion. The second is the effect that rate of increase has on the hegemon's perception of threat. Faster growth changes relative power more rapidly. Thus, the timing and extent of competition between the proto-peer and the hegemon is less predictable than it would be with a slower rate (simply

---

[1]There has been another recent attempt to model the evolution of international rivalries: Ben D. Mor and Zeev Maoz, "Learning and the Evolution of Enduring International Rivalries: A Strategic Approach," *Conflict Management and Peace Science*, 17:1 (1999), pp. 1–48. Some of the main principles of that effort (rival's satisfaction with the status quo and perceived capability to change it) resemble the assumptions of this effort.

because the margins of error of a fast rate of growth, say 7 percent a year, are greater than for a rate of 1 or 2 percent), and the hegemon must take this greater unpredictably into account. In addition, the more the proto-peer turns to external methods of increasing its power, the more directly it challenges the hegemon's rules. The combination of greater unpredictability combined with more direct challenge of the rules forces the hegemon to respond. The general rule behind the hegemon's response is that the greater the proto-peer's unpredictability and willingness to confront the rules, the more cautious the hegemon needs to be, implying a higher level of conflict imposition in the hegemon's strategy.

Two hypotheses stem from this key relationship. First, the rate at which a peer emerges results from the interaction of proto-peer and hegemon strategies. This occurs because of the direct effect the hegemon has in imposing costs on the proto-peer and because of the proto-peer's decision to potentially forgo certain paths to power aggregation because of its own risk calculation of a hegemon's punitive response. Power preponderance influences this interaction by raising the proto-peer's risks and costs for pursuing the most aggressive strategies to increase its power. In any event, a hegemon plays a major role in determining whether and how fast a peer emerges, and the role is stronger the more preponderant the hegemon.

Second, the emergence of a peer competitor has much to do with how the proto-peer became a peer. The path for transforming a proto-peer into a peer is a long one, and along it specific domestic interests are formed that, in turn, impose a certain path-dependency and restraints on the then-peer's policies. If a proto-peer becomes a peer despite a hegemon's punitive strategies, the new peer is unlikely to have the domestic interests that would favor cooperative policies toward the hegemon. If anything, such a peer might be a competitor first and a peer second. Conversely, a proto-peer that gained a peer status with support from the hegemon is likely to have the domestic interests in place that favor continuing cooperative relations. Gradually, and depending on a host of other issues, shifts toward de-escalation of tensions or toward the beginning of a rivalry may set in. However it plays out, the experience along the path to peer is formative for the proto-peer. Power preponderance makes it less likely that a proto-peer can transform into a peer against the hegemon's wishes and more likely that any peer that does make the transformation does so as a result of a cooperative policy of the hegemon. This is so because an evolution to a peer status when a preponderant hegemon actively tries to prevent or delay such an evolution is unlikely to succeed.

THE DECISION CALCULUS

With the key power growth–threat perception relationship and its two ensuring hypotheses in mind, the logic behind the evolution to a rivalry between principals in the international state system can be illustrated by use of a simple decision-tree game with two players: the hegemon and the proto-peer. Competition can take two forms: a regional-global one between a strong state seeking regional hegemony against the wishes of the global hegemon, or a global-level challenge. A challenge to the hegemon in a specific region, especially one distant from the hegemon, means that the power relations at the regional level may not be as skewed as at the global level. All of the proto-peer's capabilities can be arrayed against only a part of the hegemon's because the hegemon, by definition, has global commitments and cannot devote all of its capabilities to one region. A global-level competition assumes a regional peer.

Assume that the game starts off with a "point of notice" strategy selection, meaning that, whether because of high rates of power growth (based on the proto-peer's strategy) or because of endogenous political "shocks," the hegemon notices the proto-peer. A new actor has entered the fray and, based on an extrapolation of trends (or a power comparison, in cases of shocks leading to a point of notice), that actor has the potential to challenge the hegemon. It can challenge either in the proto-peer's region in the regional-global game or at the global hegemonic level in the global game sometime in the recognizable future (within a generation, or 20–25 years). In other words, the hegemon calculates that, based on an extrapolation of trends, the proto-peer will equal or surpass the hegemon in some important power indicators. If this condition is not met, the state in question is not a plausible proto-peer.

The hegemon then assesses sequentially the potential for a challenge from the proto-peer, based on the following set of calculations:

- Its own vulnerability to a challenge from the proto-peer (within the region in a regional-global competition or globally in a global competition);

- The proto-peer's aims;

- Its calculation of the time horizon before the proto-peer achieves parity (with parity defined as proto-peer achieving 75 percent or more of the hegemon's power within the region in a regional-global competition or at the global level in a global competition);

- The severity of a challenge.

These calculations capture the essential elements that lead to the hegemon's perception of a threat. Binary answers to each calculation cause the hegemon to adopt different strategies of hegemonic response.

The proto-peer responds to the hegemon's move by assessing sequentially the following set of calculations:

- The effect of the hegemon's strategy in constraining its pace of power growth;

- Its own satisfaction with the rules (status quo) of the international system;

- Its own proclivity toward risk taking;

- Its capability differential with the hegemon (with parity defined as the proto-peer achieving 75 percent or more of the hegemon's power within the region in a regional-global competition or at the global level in a global competition).

These calculations capture the essential elements behind the proto-peer's calculations of the most efficacious strategy of power aggregation. Binary answers to each one lead to adoption of different strategies of power growth by the proto-peer.

The game is played out using the four proto-peer and hegemon strategies, with interaction between the two governed by standard rules of rationality (actors will choose the most efficient way to achieve a goal, in a cost-benefit calculation, and based on the information available to them). Each player's projections and assessments lead it to adopt a specific strategy toward the other. Each player reassesses the situation if the other one has changed strategy and may change its own strategy accordingly. Independent of the changes induced by the other player's actions, each side is assumed to reassess constantly its own estimates of the power relationship between them and may choose a different strategy based on the revised projections.

The strategies are arrayed in a matrix, with the proto-peer strategies on the vertical axis and the hegemon's along the horizontal. They are numbered from one to four. The intersection of each pair of strategies results in one of three situations: unstable, uncertain, or quasi-equilibrium. We say "quasi-equilibrium" rather than equilibrium because the power relationship between the hegemon and the proto-peer evolves continuously, and near-term action depends on imprecise long-term projections. With the four strategies on each side arrayed in a matrix format, the diagonal line from (1,1) to (4,4) forms the set of quasi-equilibrium squares (see the shaded squares in Table 4.1) where the game may stabilize (until changes in estimates of power relationships lead to changes in strategy). Squares adjoining the quasi-equilibrium points may have temporary equilibrium, where the game may stabilize. Other squares are unstable and will necessitate a change in strategy.

Table 4.1

Proto-Peer and Hegemon Strategy Matrix

	CONCILIATE (1)	CO-OPT (2)	CONSTRAIN (3)	COMPETE (4)
CONQUEST (4)	Unstable	Unstable	Uncertain	Quasi-Equilibrium
ALLIANCE (3)	Unstable	Uncertain	Quasi-Equilibrium	Uncertain
REVOLUTION (2)	Uncertain	Quasi-Equilibrium	Uncertain	Unstable
REFORM (1)	Quasi-Equilibrium	Uncertain	Unstable	Unstable

Notation system: number designating hegemon's strategy, number designating proto-peer's strategy. Thus, Co-opt and Reform are (2,1).

Put in terms of the evolution to a rivalry, the squares in the upper right quadrant (all combinations of proto-peer and hegemon 3 and 4 strategies) are already highly conflictual and mean an existing or imminent rivalry. The squares in the lower left quadrant (all combinations of proto-peer and hegemon 1 and 2 strategies) are low in conflict and denote a pre-rivalry stage of relations.

Generally, escalation by one side provokes a response from the other because it changes some of its calculations. Thus, revisionist and aggressive moves by the proto-peer alter the hegemon's assessment of the proto-peer's aims, its own vulnerability, or the timing and severity of a threat, and they cause a hegemonic response commensurately high in conflict imposition. Similarly, a conflictual hegemonic strategy constrains a proto-peer and makes it more dissatisfied with the rules. Such an approach provokes strategies of faster power growth that may be more risky but are seen as necessary for survival. However, escalation is not automatic, as it depends on the assessment of the changed situation (according to the criteria outlined above) by the proto-peer or the hegemon. The logic for selecting some strategy matchups as equilibria and others as unstable is traced out in detail in Appendix A. As a general rule, the equilibrium line represents the approximate balance in threat perception–pace of power growth relationship.

MODELING THE INTERACTION BETWEEN A PROTO-PEER AND A HEGEMON

The simple game outlined above provides the central logic for understanding the evolution of the interaction between a proto-peer and a hegemon that might lead to competition and rivalry. To discern the deeper implications of the decision calculus outlined above, we undertook an exploratory modeling effort.

Modeling the interactions outlined above in conditions of dynamic growth and continuous change in power relations and consequent shifts in expectations and projections and on the basis of incomplete information provides several relevant insights for intelligence and policy purposes. First, it identifies more clearly the conditions leading to competition. Second, it distinguishes the pivotal player attributes from the less influential ones. Third, it reveals the potential policy impact of different assessments. Fourth, it shows how the value of intelligence assessments varies across alternative situations.

In an overall sense, the model is designed to provide a better understanding of the interaction among the decision rules in the decision-tree game. We augmented the decision rules with a notional model of ground truth and player perception. The model has initial states for each player's strategies, player attributes and perceptions, and the proto-peer's initial state power level and growth rate. The power level of the proto-peer, the actions of the two players (strategies), and player perceptions are recomputed iteratively for 20 time steps (notionally representing 20 years). The major outcome is the set of player strategies at the end of the game, which, in general, is a state of quasi-equilibrium. The pattern that emerges in these end-states after repeated runs of the model offers intelligence and policy insights.

The ground truth has several components. The first is the state power measure, expressed in arbitrary units based on the hegemon's starting level of state power. The notional aspect is that the proto-peer's power level is given a percentage (which can be varied) of the hegemon's power level, with 100 meaning parity. In the real world, arriving at this figure would entail an accurate snapshot assessment of the hegemon's absolute power and a comparison with the proto-peer.

The second component of ground truth is that the proto-peer's state power grows at a compounded rate. This annual net state power growth rate is assigned to the proto-peer and represents the pace of "catch-up," calculated after taking into account the hegemon's power growth rate and the change in the absolute levels of state power of both players. The notional aspect is that the growth rate is portrayed as a single number, established in relation to the hegemon's power level. As above, in reality, this would mean an accurate assessment of the growth trends in the hegemon's power and a comparison of the proto-peer's pace of growth.

Player actions form the third component. Actions by both players affect the growth rate of the proto-peer's power, with the hegemon's more conflictual strategies curtailing proto-peer power and the proto-peer's more aggressive growth strategies promoting it. Thus, in any given period in the model, the final growth rate is a combination of the base growth rate and an increment based on the proto-peer strategy and a decrement based on the hegemon strategy. The notional aspect is that the assessment that leads the proto-peer and the hegemon to adopt strategies is represented as ground truth and stochastic error. A player's perceptions of the other's power level are prone to error, which is modeled as an unbiased uniform stochastic process. In a given time step, the perceived power is produced by taking the true value of state power and adding a random number drawn from a uniform distribution.[2]

Finally, the interface to decision models is by way of decision attributes that are set from the other player's choice of strategy as well as the perception of the other player's overall state power level and resulting projections of future power level.

The input of information into the model is explained in more detail below. Figure 4.1 is a replica of the screen from the computer program used to run the model and displays, as a bank of slider bars, the inputs whose effects the model can explore. The initial strategies for the proto-peer and the hegemon are taken from the sets of strategies available at the start of a series of interactions. In this example, these strategies are conciliate for the hegemon and reform for the proto-peer.

Player attributes are based on the binary answers to the calculations that make up the decision calculus and lead to the adoption of a specific strategy. Rather than four attributes, only three are presented, since after the determination of an initial strategy, the hegemon's "revisionist aims" assessment and the proto-peer's "constrained" assessment change according to the other side's choice of strategy (whether it represents an escalation or de-escalation in competition). The attributes are coded as a triplet of symbols, one for each player attribute. Thus, the hegemon's attributes are input as follows:

---

[2]For example, if challenger power has the value 30 and perceptual error is 5, perceived power will be a random number drawn from a uniform distribution with range [25, 35].

Y/N (Yes/No) for "hegemon vulnerable";

L/S (Long/Short) "time horizon to parity";

Y/N (Yes/No) "threat severe."

The proto-peer's attributes are input as follows:

Y/N (Yes/No) for "constrained by hegemon's actions"

Y/N (Yes/No) for "dissatisfied with status quo";

Y/N (Yes/No) for "risk prone."

In Figure 4.1, these attributes are YLN for the hegemon (meaning: vulnerable, long time horizon, threat not severe) and YYN for the

RAND*MR1346-4.1*

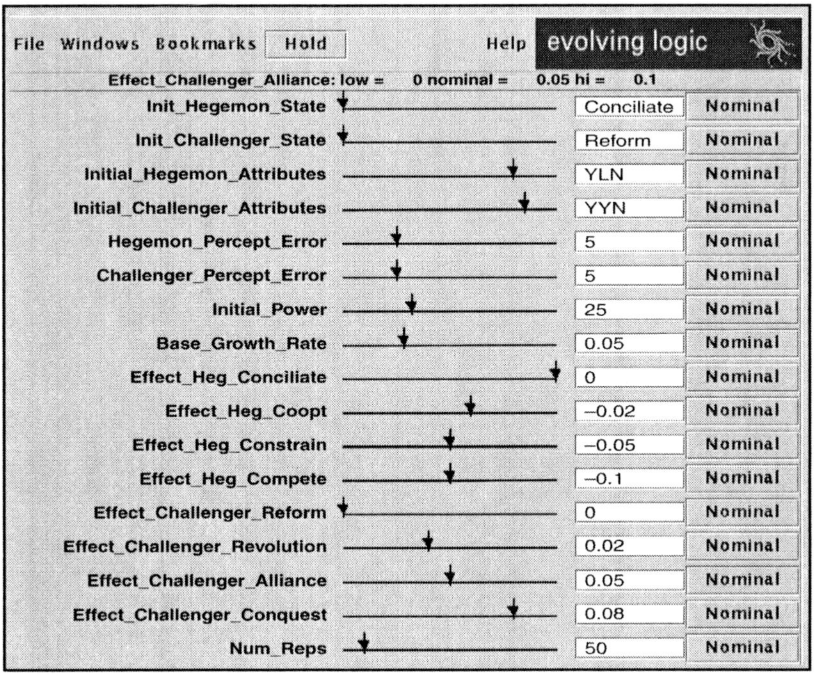

File Windows Bookmarks	Hold	Help evolving logic
Effect_Challenger_Alliance: low = 0 nominal = 0.05 hi = 0.1		
Init_Hegemon_State	Conciliate	Nominal
Init_Challenger_State	Reform	Nominal
Initial_Hegemon_Attributes	YLN	Nominal
Initial_Challenger_Attributes	YYN	Nominal
Hegemon_Percept_Error	5	Nominal
Challenger_Percept_Error	5	Nominal
Initial_Power	25	Nominal
Base_Growth_Rate	0.05	Nominal
Effect_Heg_Conciliate	0	Nominal
Effect_Heg_Coopt	−0.02	Nominal
Effect_Heg_Constrain	−0.05	Nominal
Effect_Heg_Compete	−0.1	Nominal
Effect_Challenger_Reform	0	Nominal
Effect_Challenger_Revolution	0.02	Nominal
Effect_Challenger_Alliance	0.05	Nominal
Effect_Challenger_Conquest	0.08	Nominal
Num_Reps	50	Nominal

Figure 4.1—Model Inputs

proto-peer (meaning: constrained, dissatisfied, risk prone). Moving down the menu, player perceptions designate the extent of error, expressed as a percentage, in assessment of the level of state power of the other. Here, the hegemon's and the proto-peer's perception error is set at 5 percent. The proto-peer's initial state power level is expressed as a percentage of the hegemon's state power level. In this example, the proto-peer's power level is initially set at 25 percent of the hegemon. The proto-peer's growth rate is the rate of net change in the proto-peer's power level relative to the hegemon. The growth rate here is set at 5 percent. The effect of the hegemon's strategies in decreasing the proto-peer's rate of power growth ranges from no effect with a conciliate strategy, to a mild one with a co-opt strategy, to a stronger one with a constrain strategy, and a far-reaching effect with a compete strategy (2, 5, and 10 percent, respectively, in Figure 4.1). The effect of various strategies by the proto-peer on increasing its own power growth rate also ranges from a mild increase in the rate due to a revolution strategy, to a higher one as a result of an alliance strategy, and a pronounced increase due to a conquest strategy (2, 5, and 8 percent, respectively). The number of repetitions for the specific run of the model based on the characteristics outlined in the given window is the last entry on the screen (50 in this example—the last line in Figure 4.1). Performing the repetitions aimed at capturing the recurring patterns rather than relying on a single (and perhaps misleading) run of the model. The values shown are the nominal values for all of the inputs, which are the values used for subsequent graphs, except where explicitly noted.

The rules for determining the hegemon's and the proto-peer's perceptions, showing how some of the concepts that comprise the players' attributes are operationalized, are summarized in Tables 4.2 and 4.3. Table 4.4 shows the rules for the hegemon's assessment of the proto-peer as being revisionist, and Table 4.5 shows the rules for the proto-peer's assessment of being constrained. Both assessments are important components of the decision to escalate or de-escalate.

Finally, Tables 4.6 and 4.7 show the hegemon and proto-peer rules for a strategy decision, respectively. Appendix B provides the full code for the model.

Table 4.2

Summary of Hegemon Perception Rules

Assessment of vulnerability to a challenge from a proto-peer: Yes/No
• Unchanging over time (explore as an input)
Assessment of proto-peer's aims, revisionist or not: Yes/No
• Initial value input, changes with proto-peer's escalation or de-escalation of strategies, or if proto-peer fails to follow hegemon's escalation or de-escalation
Calculation of time horizon to proto-peer achieving parity: Long/Short
• Projected time to parity is calculated on the basis of a linear extrapolation of perceived proto-peer power level over last 2 years;
• Long, if time to parity > 20 yrs & proto-peer state is 1 or 2, or if time to parity > 30 yrs & proto-peer state is 3 or 4;
• Short otherwise
Assessment of severity of proto-peer's challenge, severe or not: Yes/No
• No, if time to parity > 10 years & proto-peer state is 1 or 2, or if time to parity > 20 years & proto-peer state is 3 or 4;
• Yes otherwise

Table 4.3

Summary of Proto-Peer Perception Rules

Assessment of impact of hegemon's strategy in constraining own power growth, constrained or not: Yes/No
• Initial value input, changes with hegemon escalation or de-escalation
Extent of satisfaction with the rules of the international system, satisfied or not: Yes/No
• Unchanging over time (explore as an input)
Proclivity toward risk-taking, risk prone or not (risk averse): Yes/No
• Unchanging over time (explore as an input)
Assessment of capability differential with the hegemon, presence of major differential or not: Yes/No
• No, if perceived proto-peer power relative to hegemon > 75 & hegemon state is 1 or 2, or if perceived proto-peer power > 50 & hegemon state is 3 or 4;
• Yes otherwise

Table 4.4

Hegemon Perception Rules in Assessment of "Revisionism"

• If proto-peer escalated on last move, "Aims Revisionist" becomes YES
• If proto-peer de-escalated on last move, "Aims Revisionist" becomes NO
• If proto-peer did neither on last move in response to hegemon escalation, then "Aims Revisionist" becomes NO
• If proto-peer did neither on last move in response to hegemon de-escalation, then "Aims Revisionist" becomes YES
• If proto-peer did neither on last move and proto-peer strategy is "reform," then "Aims Revisionist" becomes NO
• Otherwise "Aims Revisionist" is unchanged

Table 4.5

Proto-Peer Perception Rules in Assessment of Being "Constrained"

• If hegemon escalated on last move, then "Constrained" becomes YES
• If hegemon de-escalated on last move "Constrained" becomes NO
• If hegemon did neither on last move in response to proto-peer escalation, then "Constrained" becomes NO
• If hegemon did neither on last move in response to proto-peer de-escalation, then "Constrained" becomes YES
• If hegemon did neither on last move and hegemon strategy is "Conciliate," then "Constrained" becomes NO
• Otherwise "Constrained" is unchanged

Table 4.6

Rules for Hegemon Strategy Decision

• If "Vulnerable" is NO, then de-escalate unless hegemon already de-escalated on last move
• If "Vulnerable" is YES, and "Aims Revisionist" is NO, play same level as proto-peer
• If "Vulnerable" is YES, and "Aims Revisionist" is YES, and "Time Horizon" is LONG, escalate 1 step (but not higher than 3)
• If "Vulnerable" is YES, and "Aims Revisionist" is YES, and "Time Horizon" is SHORT, then: if "Threat Severe" is NO, escalate 2 steps   if "Threat Severe" is YES escalate 3 steps (go directly to 4 = Compete)

Note: de-escalation below 1 or escalation above 4 cannot occur.

Table 4.7

Rules for Proto-Peer Strategy Decision

• If "Constrained" is NO, then de-escalate unless Challenger already de-escalated last move
• If "Constrained" is YES, but "Dissatisfied" is NO, strategy remains unchanged
• If "Constrained" is YES and "Dissatisfied" is YES, but "Risk Prone" is NO, escalate by 1 (but don't go above 3 unless Capability Differential is NO)
• If "Constrained," "Dissatisfied," and "Risk Prone" are YES: if "Capability Differential" is YES, go to 3 = Alliance if "Capability Differential" is NO, go to 4 = Conquest

Note: de-escalation below 1 or escalation above 4 cannot occur.

The model supports an exploration of a variety of factors. On the basis of the full range of hegemon and proto-peer initial strategies and attributes, it allows for manipulation of the rates of perception error by the hegemon and the proto-peer, the proto-peer's initial state power level, the proto-peer's growth rate, and the extent of the effects of all the strategies by both the proto-peer and the hegemon upon the proto-peer's growth rate.

Effect of Perceptual Errors

Except for perceptual error, the model described here is completely deterministic, and would behave identically if run twice with the same inputs. The behavior of the players depends upon their perception of the current situation. They perceive changes in each other's strategy accurately, but the assessment of their relative power differential (based as it is on an intelligence process) is prone to error.

So, perceptual errors make the model stochastic and are represented by pseudo-random draws from a uniform and symmetric distribution about ground truth and whose range is a model input variable. Figure 4.2 shows the average behavior over 50 Monte Carlo draws (for the "nominal" case shown in Figure 4.1, where the perceptual errors are 5 percent). Perceptual error introduces variability and results in fractional values in the average.

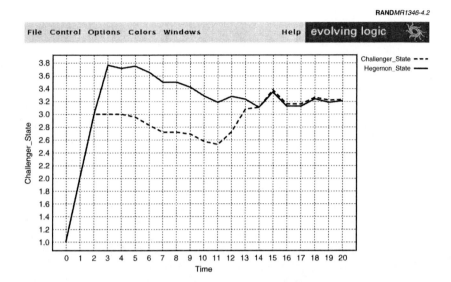

Figure 4.2—Effect of Perceptual Error

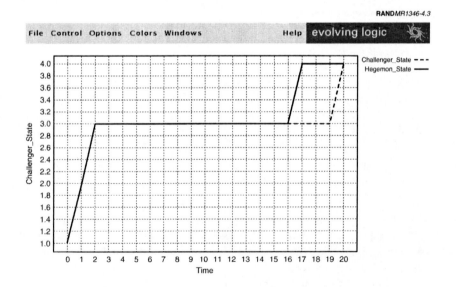

Figure 4.3—Outcomes with No Perceptual Error

In contrast, setting the perceptual error for both the hegemon and the proto-peer to zero results in the time series shown in Figure 4.3. The pure integers reflected here result from identical behavior on each Monte Carlo trial. Trajectories of this type will be seen for each case that makes up the stochastic behaviors shown in Figure 4.1.

The pattern of outcomes across the 50 cases that average to the curve shown in Figure 4.2 cannot in general be determined without examining the actual trajectories in each case. And the explanation for each such trajectory requires walking through the logic of the decision rules for each time step in each case. To understand the implications of the decision rules, in the remainder of this section we combine the examination of the details in specific cases with empirical documentation of the observed behavior of the model across ranges of behavior for cases of interest.

Figures 4.4 and 4.5 illustrate how the introduction of a minor assessment error into the model can lead to an adoption of a more competitive strategy. For example, taking an initial 2,1 situation (co-opt and reform), all other values as shown in Figure 4.1, and with no errors in perception, the proto-peer–hegemon interaction quickly stabilizes at the 3,3 level (see Figure 4.4).

More specifically, on turn 1, the hegemon perceives itself vulnerable to a revisionist state in the long run and escalates its strategy to constrain, moving from a 2 to a 3. The proto-peer escalates in turn to a revolution strategy, moving from a 1 to a 2. On turn 2, the hegemon does not escalate in response to the proto-peer's escalation because the time horizon for a threat is long. It retains the constrain strategy. The proto-peer escalates to alliance. The hegemon does not escalate further, nor does the proto-peer. In fact, there are no further moves and the game remains at 3,3. As long as the time horizon for the hegemon's vulnerability remains long, the hegemon does not escalate above the constrain strategy. The hegemon's strategy is effective enough in depressing the proto-peer's growth rate so that the long time frame for a challenge to materialize remains in place.

On the other hand, the proto-peer does not escalate above the alliance strategy as long as the hegemon retains the constrain strategy and as long as a large difference in capabilities remains. Although the relations between the two are predominantly conflictual, the

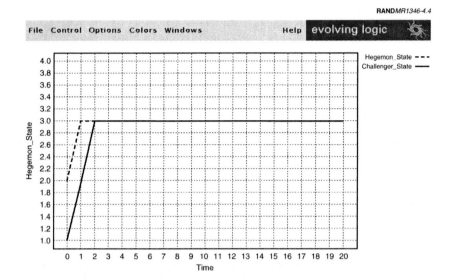

Figure 4.4—Example of a 2,1 Game with No Perceptual Error

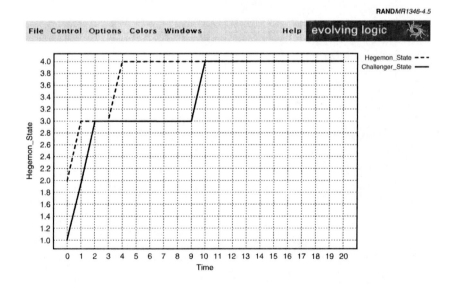

Figure 4.5—Example of a 2,1 Game with Perceptual Error

hegemon succeeds in suppressing the power growth of the proto-peer. The proto-peer, though revisionist, does not emerge into a peer.

The same starting situation results in a higher level of competition when a perception error is factored into the model. The first two moves are the same as in the nonerror case. But then, rather than stopping at the 3,3 level, the game continues to escalate to the 4,4 level (see Figure 4.5).

On game turn 4, perception error causes the hegemon to project the proto-peer to achieve parity within 20 years (because the proto-peer is pursuing an aggressive alliance strategy, the time frame of 20, rather than 10, is taken as a short time frame; see Table 4.2), resetting the perceived time horizon to short and causing the hegemon to escalate to compete strategy. The proto-peer does not escalate for a while, leading to a 4,3 game. Then, after some change in the respective power level, on turn 10 the proto-peer calculates its power level to be within 25 percent of parity, leading to an assessment that the capability differential is no longer major and causing the proto-peer to escalate to a strategy of conquest. The proto-peer's calculation that leads to escalation is based on an error in perception. The game stabilizes at a highly competitive 4,4 level, with a high potential for an armed conflict.

It must be noted that in contrast with Figure 4.2, which averages over 50 stochastic cases and hence shows fractional states, Figures 4.4 and 4.5 show single cases. Consequently, each player has an integral state at every time step. These two figures can be interpreted as alternative outcomes that could plausibly result from different random "coin flips" of perceptual error. In what follows, we examine in greater depth the effects that perceptual error can have on the shape of the competition.

IDENTIFYING THE ATTRIBUTES THAT LEAD TO COMPETITION AND RIVALRY

The model provides insight into what player attributes lead to escalation and potential conflict. We used the model to analyze the final outcomes of all possible combinations of attributes and all possible strategy matches at the pre-rivalry stage (that is, four combinations, two proto-peer and two hegemon, of reform, revolution, conciliate, and co-opt). The four figures below portray the final states for the hegemon and the proto-peer along these lines (since the final strategy choices for the proto-peer and the hegemon are identical in all four cases, only one screen is shown), with Figure 4.6 showing the conciliate/reform (1,1) initial situation, Figure 4.7 the co-opt/reform (2,1) starting situation, Figure 4.8 the conciliate/revolution (1,2) initial situation, and Figure 4.9 the co-opt/revolution (2,2) starting situation. All other inputs are nominal.

The notation system for player attributes follows the triplet of symbols, one for each attribute, explained earlier. The hegemon attributes are: whether the hegemon is "vulnerable," the initial value for the "time horizon to parity," and the initial hegemon assessment of "severity of threat." The proto-peer attributes, from left to right, are: whether the proto-peer is "constrained" (modified based on game play in subsequent moves), whether the proto-peer is "dissatisfied" with the status quo, and whether the proto-peer is "risk prone."

Initial player attributes have a large effect on the final outcome, and the general pattern that emerges in the pre-rivalry final outcomes is that escalation occurs when attribute combinations are a mixture of the proto-peer being dissatisfied and the hegemon being vulnerable. Specific initial situation characteristics provide more nuances in this pattern. The pattern of dissatisfied and vulnerable being dangerous holds in (1,1) and (2,1) initial situations, with the only difference being that in the (2,1) situation the level of escalation of the hegemon attributes of YSN is higher (3.1 compared with 2.9).

An initial situation of (1,2) leads to the same pattern as in (1,1), with the exception of a final state of a vulnerable hegemon and a satisfied peer (Y and N respectively). This situation results in values of 2 in the bottom two boxes of the last four columns (medium gray fill). These values were 1 in the (1,1) initial scenario.

Another clear pattern is that in all four initial pre-rivalry situations, the initial value of proto-peer power matters. Figure 4.10 shows the relation between initial proto-peer power and probability of conflict for the nominal case ((1,1), with a volatile mix of attributes). When the proto-peer does not have much power relative to the hegemon,

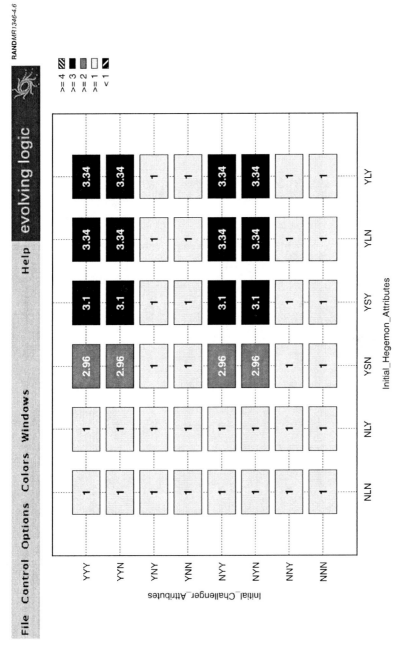

Figure 4.6—Final Player States, (1,1) Initial Situation

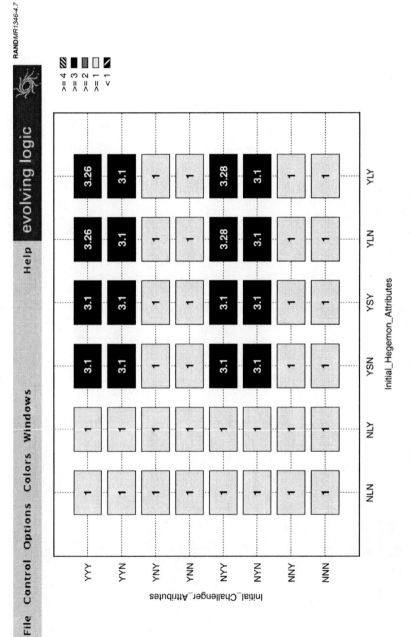

Figure 4.7—Final Player States, (2,1) Initial Situation

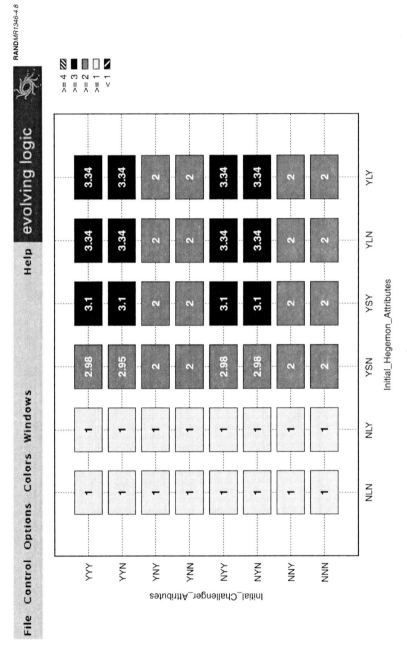

Figure 4.8—Final Player Attributes, (1,2) Initial Situation

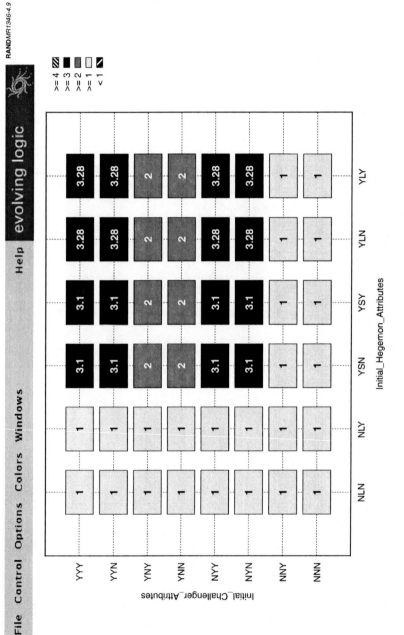

Figure 4.9—Final Player Attributes, (2,2) Initial Situation

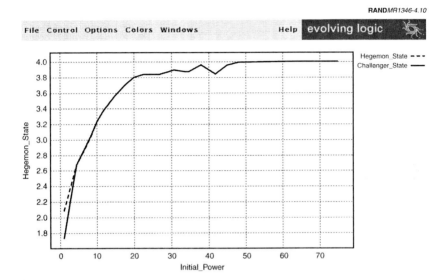

**Figure 4.10—Impact of Initial Proto-Peer Level of State Power on
Probability of a Highly Conflictual Final Outcome**

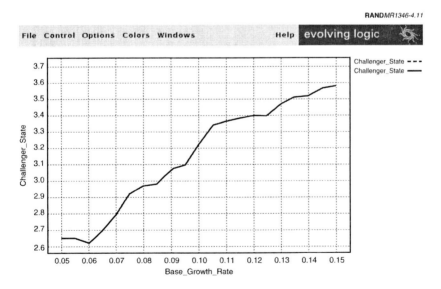

**Figure 4.11—Impact of Proto-Peer Base Growth Rate on Probability of a
Highly Conflictual Final Outcome**

the probability of conflict is low. But as power increases, the probability of conflict rises sharply. For example, the nominal value for initial power of 10 yields an average final state of 3.2 (which corresponds to the value shown in Figure 4.6). Past 50, a highly conflictual outcome is certain.

Similarly, the proto-peer's base growth rate also has the impact of increasing the probability of a highly conflictual situation, although the growth's influence on the final state is more gradual than in the case of initial power level. Figure 4.11 shows the relationship for the nominal case, with the slope clearly more gradual than the slope in Figure 4.10.

The model illustrates that perceptual error can sometimes have a major influence on the eventual outcome. But an interesting pattern that emerges is the different extent of the influence of perceptual error, depending on which player commits it. Hegemon perceptual error has a relatively more pronounced impact on the outcome than does proto-peer perceptual error.

Figures 4.12 and 4.13 illustrate the difference. Figure 4.12 shows the graph of final outcomes for initial hegemon attributes YSY (vulnerable, short time horizon, threat severe), with all other parameters being nominal. Depending on the extent of hegemon perceptual error, the expected outcome can range from peaceful (1,1) to conflictual (4,4), a spread of three points. In the identical case, illustrated in Figure 4.13, where the hegemon perceptual error is nominal (5 percent), the range of final outcomes for the proto-peer only ranges from 2 to 3. Thus, the proto-peer's perceptual error matters, but not as much as the hegemon's.

For this model, the sign of the effect of perceptual error also depends on the actor. For both actors, errors of underestimation and overestimation are equally likely. (We have intentionally used the most simplistic model possible for perceptual error. In a more in-depth analysis, this aspect of the model representation deserves further investigation.) However, the nature of the decision rules causes the effects of over- and underestimation of the power differential to be different for the two sides. For the hegemon, errors that make the threat appear more severe can often result in escalation in the level of conflict that would not occur without the error, and this escalation

Figure 4.12—Impact of Hegemon Perceptual Error in Increasing the
Probability of a Highly Conflictual Final Outcome

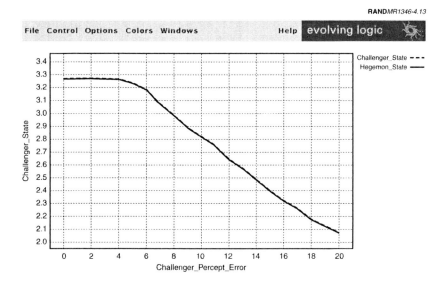

Figure 4.13—Impact of Proto-Peer Perceptual Error in Increasing the
Probability of a Highly Conflictual Final Outcome

can be hard to reverse. Errors that underestimate the threat have more complex effects; such an error may lessen the likelihood of conflict in the near term, but the failure to constrain the challenger's growth can result in the same or even greater escalation later when the error is realized.

For the challenger, overestimating its strength could result in premature challenge, causing the hegemon to constrain its growth earlier than otherwise would have occurred, and the overall result will depend upon the details of the case. Overestimating the power differential, on the other hand, will tend to cause the challenger to be more conservative, which tends uniformly to result in lower levels of competition.

On balance, Figures 4.12 and 4.13 demonstrate that for this model, hegemon perceptual error tends to increase the level of conflict while challenger error decreases it. Given the notional representation of the perceptual process used here, caution is appropriate in drawing conclusions from this observation. Other assumptions about the intelligence process could conceivably alter this conclusion. By contrast, the observations that perceptual error can have a major impact on the level of competition and that the size of the effect will be situation-dependent are much more likely to hold for any alternative model of perception.

In fact, in the specific case illustrated in Figures 4.12 and 4.13, the decisiveness of the hegemon's perceptual error in triggering escalatory dynamics is even more pronounced than the graphics suggest. The case has an instability, with only a final state of (1,1) or (4,4) ever occurring (averages of 2 or 3 on previous graphs result from a mix of (1,1) and (4,4) final outcomes). Figure 4.14 shows two intersecting curves. They show the percentage of (1,1) or (4,4) outcomes that occur as a result of hegemon error. No error yields 100 percent (1,1) outcomes. The percentage of (1,1) final outcomes decreases quickly from 100 percent to 5 percent as hegemon perceptual error increases from 0 to 20 percent. Conversely, the percentage of (4,4) final outcomes quickly increases from 0 to 95 percent over the same range. The results in this specific case illustrate vividly that in some situations, accurate assessments of the proto-peer by the hegemon make the difference between peaceful accommodation and a conflict-prone rivalry.

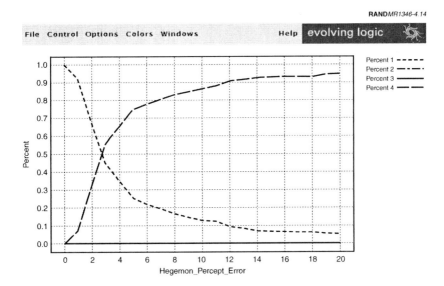

Figure 4.14—In Some Situations Perceptual Error Has Decisive Impact on Probability of a Highly Conflictual Final Outcome

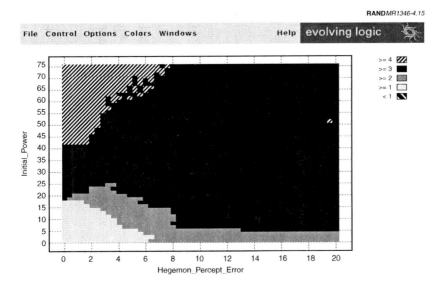

Figure 4.15—Impact of Proto-Peer Base Growth Rate on Probability of a Highly Conflictual Final Outcome

However, it is important to note that the importance of hegemon perceptual error depends on the situation. In the specific case illustrated in Figures 4.12 to 4.14, hegemon perceptual error matters only when the proto-peer's initial power level is assessed at less than 20. And even in those cases, the acceptable level of error varies with the actual situation. Figure 4.15 shows this outcome by identifying a region plot of final state as a function of hegemon error and initial power for the same case considered in Figures 4.12 to 4.14.[3] The strong impact of situation-specific circumstances is generally true and makes universal statements about the value of assessments of the other player difficult to evaluate. However, conditional evaluations are clearly possible.

Player attributes play a role in sensitivity to error (the likelihood that error will have a strategy-altering effect). As a general pattern, in the prerivalry initial cases, sensitivity is greatest when the proto-peer is dissatisfied and risk prone and the hegemon is vulnerable but initially believes the time horizon is long. Using the nominal case, Figures 4.16 to 4.18 illustrate this pattern of sensitivity to error, based on the various combinations of player attributes and depending on the initial situation. Figure 4.16 does so for the (1,1) initial situation, Figure 4.17 does the same for the (2,1) starting situation, and Figure 4.18 for the (2,2) initial situation.

The pattern just described holds primarily with respect to weaker proto-peers. The more powerful the proto-peer in the initial situation, the greater the sensitivity to perception error, and the greatest sensitivity to perception error shifts to a situation where the proto-peer is dissatisfied but not risk prone. Figure 4.19 illustrates this change by coding the initial proto-peer power level as 50.

---

[3]Note that these region plots are created through a series of shadings, where values of 4 or greater (which means exactly 4.0) are cross-hatch, values greater or equal to 3.0 but less that 4.0 are the next shading (black), values greater than or equal to 2.0 but less than 3.0 are medium gray, etc. This means that values of 2.1 and 2.9 will both be medium gray on this chart, and 2.99 will be medium gray while 3.0 will be black. Thus, the isolated cross-hatch spot on the right-hand side of Figure 4.15 is a stochastic effect of all cases where initial power is greater than 40 being nearly 4.0, where only those that are exactly 4.0 are cross-hatch, with nearby values (for example, 3.9) shown as black. This is an unavoidable effect of using shading schemes, requiring care in interpreting such diagrams. Used together with other forms of display, the meaning of such figures can be made clear.

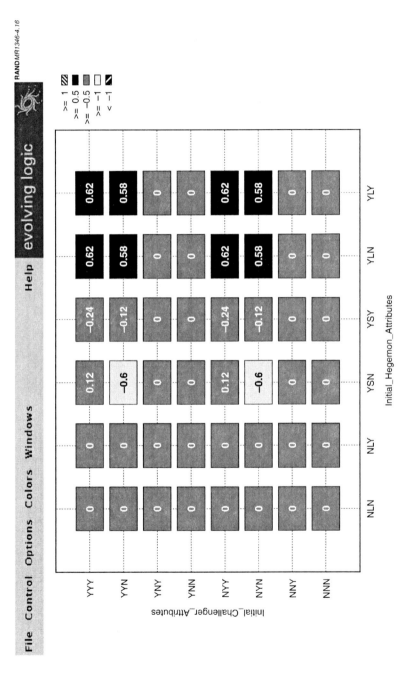

Figure 4.16—Sensitivity to Error, (1,1) Initial Situation

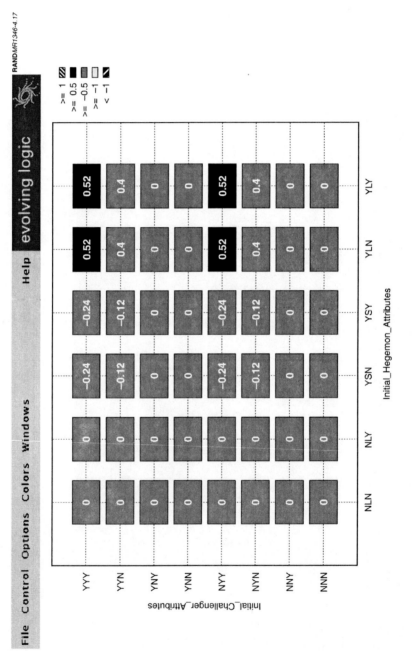

Figure 4.17—Sensitivity to Error, (2,1) Initial Situation

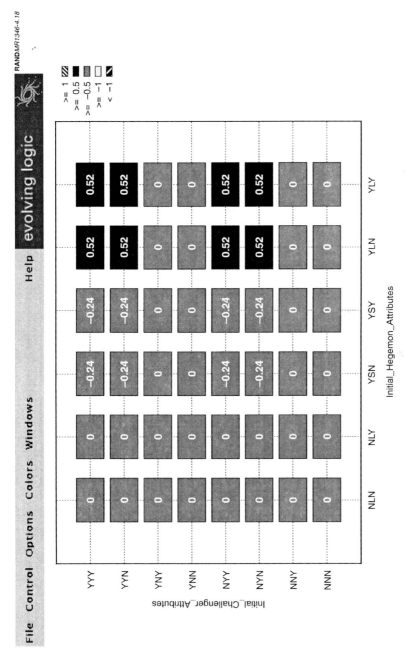

Figure 4.18—Sensitivity to Error, (2,2) Initial Situation

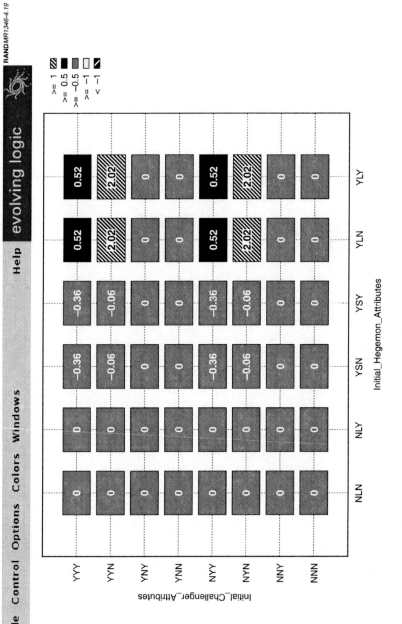

Figure 4.19—Sensitivity to Perceptual Error, Initial Proto-Peer Power Level = 50

A similar kind of a shift toward greater impact of error with higher initial proto-peer power level also takes place as the hegemon adopts more conflictual strategies toward the proto-peer. Figures 4.20 and 4.21 show the impact of perceptual error, based on the initial situation and initial power levels of the proto-peer. Figure 4.20 graphs the impact of error for the (1,1) initial situation, and Figure 4.21 does so for the (2,1) starting situation. The two graphs have a similar shape, though there is a pronounced rightward shift (toward a higher initial proto-peer power level) in the impact of perception error in the (2,1) situation.

FINAL OBSERVATIONS AND CAVEATS REGARDING THE MODEL

The prototype model presented here illustrates the potential of this approach to thinking about hegemon-peer rivalry. The model provides insight into several important phenomena. First, the model distinguishes between stable and unstable strategic relations between a proto-peer and the hegemon. Second, it identifies a number of results from the interaction between the hegemon and a proto-peer, some intuitive and some not. For example, dissatisfaction on the part of the proto-peer with the rules of the international system as a strong indicator of potential for escalation to a rivalry is not surprising. Neither are a strong starting position for a proto-peer or a high growth rate. But the model's ability to identify situation-specific conditions that may or may not lead to competition and rivalry when the other more obvious elements are present is a notable contribution. For example, the model takes into account the role that regime leadership may play in otherwise competitively inclined potential proto-peer regimes by incorporating the regime's propensity for risk into the interaction. Third, the model incorporates the effect of assessment error on the part of both the hegemon and the proto-peer in leading to strategic escalation and potential rivalry. The patterns identified by the model—for example the relatively larger effect of hegemon error in certain situations, the situation-specific correlation of attributes of the hegemon and proto-peer and their sensitivity to error, or the shift in error sensitivity when the proto-peer is initially strong—provide insights into the role of intelligence assessments in leading to the adoption of specific strategies. Moreover, the model demonstrated variability in the

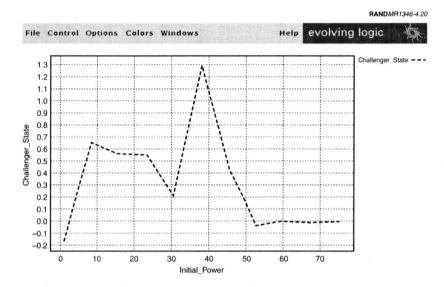

Figure 4.20—Impact of Error, by Initial Proto-Peer Power Level, (1,1) Initial Situation

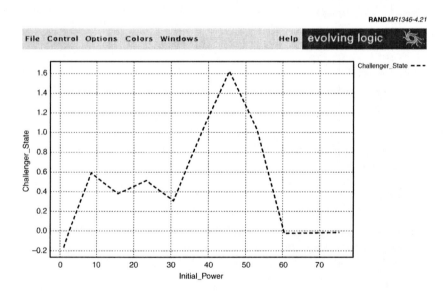

Figure 4.21—Impact of Error, by Initial Proto-Peer Power Level, (2,1) Initial Situation

value of intelligence assessments across alternative situations. The model shows potential for assessing the impact of potential error in intelligence estimates.

However, there are important caveats regarding the model. Most of all, the model is notional in several respects, especially as it treats the proto-peer's power level and its growth in power, and in its consideration of perception and the intelligence assessment of the other actor. At this stage, the model is not a forecasting but a reasoning tool useful for understanding the implications of the decision rules. As such, the results presented here should not be interpreted as empirical, because they are not. They are a step toward a systematic understanding of the structure and the processes of the circumstances that might lead to a rivalry between principals in the international system.

Further Development of the Model

Based on the encouraging initial results, there are a number of potentially profitable ways to expand on the prototype model presented here.

One, validation of the model (and its underlying framework) is a necessary step before proceeding further. The decision rules are logically derived, but they need to be tested against historical examples to ensure their applicability. Including alternative rationality logic (such as suggested by certain combinations stemming from the use of prospect theory) could complement the logic used in this report and would be one way to deal with seemingly less-than-rational actors. Overall, validation activities might lead to further development of the notional aspects of the model, especially as they pertain to assessment and perception.

Two, the model's realism (and consequently its complexity) could be increased. The potential pathways for doing so include expanding the choices of strategies, providing for hedging strategies, possibly allowing for greater de-escalation, or adding additional areas for perception error. The model also could be expanded to take into account several players, rather than the current two. A four- or five-actor model is feasible.

Three, the model could be developed into an operational tool producing reliable outputs. Such a tool would be adapted to a specific case rather than being generic in its current form. To do this, the useful properties of such a tool would have to be better understood.

Four, the framework presented here, if developed further and combined with a model grounded in a real situation, could provide a useful basis for robust decisionmaking by assisting in intelligence estimates. It could help allocate intelligence resources to situations that most need accuracy or that have the greatest leverage on outcomes and in the establishment of parameters for acceptable range of error in intelligence estimates. At a more practical level, the model could serve as an early-warning tool to suggest signposts of potentially unstable situations and to inform debates between alternative stances in dealing with potential competitors. The model could be developed to a point where it would allow methods for combining multiple estimates of state power in a fashion that incorporates the potential consequences of error.

Chapter Five

CONCLUSIONS

The theoretical and modeling efforts presented in this report provide a systematic understanding of the interaction between a proto-peer and the hegemon that might lead to any number of final states, ranging from accommodation to rivalry. The specific utility of the theoretical and modeling efforts is to structure the analysis, view the interaction as a process, and to note the important role of error in assessment in leading to the adoption of inefficient (unnecessarily costly) policies.

Predicting a competition well before a state becomes a peer is exceedingly difficult. The long time horizons associated with such predictions and the inability of contemporary forecasting tools to predict nonlinear change[1] virtually ensure an unacceptably high margin of error. Modeling the decision structure available to the proto-peer and the hegemon offers a possible alternative to the more traditional approaches.

The theoretical and modeling work presented in this report leads to at least three inferences regarding the potential for the emergence of a peer competitor (each of which is discussed in more detail below):

- U.S. preponderance of power makes the emergence of a peer competitor unlikely in the near future.

---

[1]Robert U. Ayres, "On Forecasting Discontinuities," *Technological Forecasting and Social Change*, 65:1 (September 2000), pp. 81–97.

- The most likely route for the emergence of a peer competitor any time soon is by way of an alliance.

- Errors in a hegemon's assessment of a proto-peer are more critical than errors in assessment of a hegemon by a proto-peer.

Regarding the first point, at the most general level, given the preponderance of power that the United States currently has, the emergence of a peer competitor any time soon would stem as much from U.S. actions as it would from those of potential peers. Power preponderance lessens the age-old hegemon problem of having to walk a fairly narrow line between conciliation and conflict, both of which can speed the growth of a peer competitor. The United States can still either delay the emergence of a peer or try to moderate a proto-peer's potential competitive tendencies, but the extent of current power preponderance allows it to err on the side of caution and try to use less conflictual and more positive incentives.

On the other hand, the conditions of power preponderance constrain further a proto-peer's already difficult balancing act of needing to pursue policies that enable it to aggregate power without simultaneously alarming the United States. There are incentives in place for proto-peers to pursue internally focused and less threatening strategies that lead to slower power growth and strengthen the domestic interests in favor of accommodation with the United States.

The above assumes the existence of the widely accepted power preponderance. But what if the extent of U.S. preponderance is not as great as most defense analysts believe? The modeling effort illustrates the role of error in assessment and its potential to lead to unnecessary escalation and potential rivalry that would be difficult to undo. Moreover, the model illustrates that in certain situations, too much conciliation can speed the growth of a competitor, and that pattern is more pronounced the more powerful the proto-peer is at the outset of an analysis. Barry Buzan referred to a similar phenomenon in discussing the potential for a conciliatory policy being a double-edged sword in U.S. policy toward China:

> To pursue trade and investment with [China] is to gamble that the liberal logic of interdependence and domestic transformation (from market to democracy) will work more quickly and powerfully than the realist logic of foolishly strengthening an opponent that you

> may one day have to fight. The inconsistencies of American policy towards China . . . illustrate the difficulties of choice, and perhaps nowhere does this liberal-realist dilemma operate more clearly than in relation to a potential superpower such as China. By engaging with the Chinese economy Asian and Western traders and investors enrich themselves and China, and entangle Beijing in the liberal incentive scheme of joint gains requiring peaceful relations. But by enriching a still authoritarian China, and upgrading its technological capacity and economic weight, they also make it more powerful, increasing its means to make trouble should its leaders want to go in that direction.[2]

As for the second point, assessment error aside, even in conditions of current U.S. power preponderance, the fact remains that if three or more other major states of the world were to coalesce against it, the United States might be faced with something akin to a peer competitor. Similarly, the breakdown of the U.S. alliance system in Europe and/or east Asia and the potential emergence of former allies as competitors would change radically the strategic position of the United States in the world. Both types of change would amount to an endogenous shock to the power hierarchy in the international state system and reduce the relative power dominance of the United States. At any one moment, such events seem unlikely, but over time the probability increases of such a change occurring. That long-term increase in probability should serve as a reminder that the hegemon's old problem of choosing the right mix of conciliation and conflict may have lessened in intensity for the United States (given its power preponderance), but it remains in place. Given the U.S. position at the apex of the international power hierarchy, it matters greatly how it upholds the rules or establishes new ones for the international state system in terms of the levels of satisfaction with the system that proto-peers may have. At stake is the potential for a proto-peer to metamorphose into a "principal rival," reminiscent of the Cold War.

As to the third point, perhaps the most important inference that can be drawn from the modeling work presented here for U.S. defense policy is the importance of accurate intelligence assessments and the

---

[2]Barry Buzan, "'Change and Insecurity' Reconsidered," *Contemporary Security Policy,* 20:3 (December 1999), pp. 13–14.

need for the intelligence community to recognize the extent of acceptable error in its assessments of a proto-peer. On the basis of the research reported here, it is possible to construct a tool that would be suited to analysis of the potential error in assessment and the likely impact of error in that assessment on decisionmaking and policy.

DECISION RULES

Proto-Peer and Hegemon Strategy Matrix

	CONCILIATE (1)	CO-OPT (2)	CONSTRAIN (3)	COMPETE (4)
CONQUEST (4)	Unstable	Unstable	Uncertain	Quasi-Equilibrium
ALLIANCE (3)	Unstable	Uncertain	Quasi-Equilibrium	Uncertain
REVOLUTION (2)	Uncertain	Quasi-Equilibrium	Uncertain	Unstable
REFORM (1)	Quasi-Equilibrium	Uncertain	Unstable	Unstable

Notation system: number designating hegemon's strategy, number designating proto-peer's strategy. Thus, Co-opt and Reform are (2,1).

GAME STARTING FROM (1,1), ALL POSSIBLE PATHWAYS

Sequential game, hegemon (H or Heg) moves first, based on an evaluation of the proto-peer (P or P-p).

See Figure A.1 for a graphic presentation of the decision tree.

****

H: NO

Heg: vulnerable?

NO

Decision tree stops. Game remains at 1,1 (no need to go to proto-peer response because no change in strategy by hegemon)

RESULT: 1,1

****

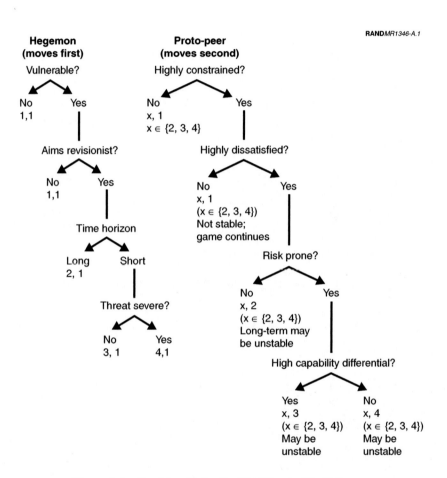

RAND*MR1346-A.1*

Figure A.1—Decision Rules for First Turn of (x,1) Game

H: YES, NO

Heg: vulnerable?

YES

Decision tree goes on to a second set of questions:

Heg: are aims of proto-peer revisionist?

NO

Decision tree stops. Game remains at 1,1 (no need to go to proto-peer response because no change in strategy by hegemon)

RESULT: 1,1

****

H: YES, YES, LONG; P: NO

Heg: vulnerable?

YES

Decision tree goes on to a second set of questions:

Heg: are aims of proto-peer revisionist?

YES

Decision tree goes on to a third set of questions:

Heg: what is the time horizon for a challenge to appear?

LONG

Hegemon changes strategy toward proto-peer to 2 (co-opt), leading to a current interaction of strategies: 2,1. The game now goes on to the proto-peer, to evaluate whether the proto-peer will change its own strategy as a result of a new strategy by the hegemon.

P-p: Has the change in the hegemon's strategy placed high constraints on the proto-peer?

NO

Decision tree stops. Game remains at 2,1 (no need to go to hegemon response because no change in strategy by proto-peer)

RESULT: 2,1

****

H: YES, YES, LONG; P: YES, NO

Heg: vulnerable?

YES

Decision tree goes on to a second set of questions:

Heg: are aims of proto-peer revisionist?

YES

Decision tree goes on to a third set of questions:

Heg: what is the time horizon for a challenge to appear?

LONG

Hegemon changes strategy toward proto-peer to 2 (co-opt), leading to a current interaction of strategies: 2,1. The game now goes on to the proto-peer, to evaluate whether the proto-peer will change its own strategy as a result of a new strategy by the hegemon.

P-p: Has the change in the hegemon's strategy placed high constraints on the proto-peer?

YES

Decision tree goes on to a second set of proto-peer's questions:

P-p: Is the proto-peer highly dissatisfied?

NO

Decision tree stops. Game remains at 2,1 (no need to go to hegemon response because no change in strategy by proto-peer)

RESULT: 2,1

****

H: YES, YES, LONG; P: YES, YES, NO; (H: cont)

Heg: vulnerable?

YES

Decision tree goes on to a second set of questions:

Heg: are aims of proto-peer revisionist?

YES

Decision tree goes on to a third set of questions:

Heg: what is the time horizon for a challenge to appear?

LONG

Hegemon changes strategy toward proto-peer to 2 (co-opt), leading to a current interaction of strategies: 2,1. The game now goes on to the proto-peer, to evaluate whether the proto-peer will change its own strategy as a result of a new strategy by the hegemon.

P-p: Has the change in the hegemon's strategy placed high constraints on the proto-peer?

YES

Decision tree goes on to a second set of proto-peer's questions:

P-p: Is the proto-peer highly dissatisfied?

YES

Decision tree goes on to a third set of proto-peer's questions:

P-p: Is the proto-peer risk prone?

NO

Proto-peer changes strategy toward hegemon to 2 (revolution), leading to a current interaction of strategies: 2,2. The game now goes back to the hegemon, to evaluate whether the hegemon will change its own strategy as a result of a new strategy by the proto-peer. Hegemon goes back to the same decision tree choices but now fed with different information and with different assessments.

Heg: . . . [RESULT: continue playing as if starting point is 2,2]

****

H: YES, YES, LONG; P: YES, YES, YES, YES; (H: cont)

Heg: vulnerable?

YES

Decision tree goes on to a second set of questions:

Heg: are aims of proto-peer revisionist?

YES

Decision tree goes on to a third set of questions:

Heg: what is the time horizon for a challenge to appear?

LONG

Hegemon changes strategy toward proto-peer to 2 (co-opt), leading to a current interaction of strategies: 2,1. The game now goes on to the proto-peer, to evaluate whether the proto-peer will change its own strategy as a result of a new strategy by the hegemon.

P-p: Has the change in the hegemon's strategy placed high constraints on the proto-peer?

YES

Decision tree goes on to a second set of proto-peer's questions:

P-p: Is the proto-peer highly dissatisfied?

YES

Decision tree goes on to a third set of proto-peer's questions:

P-p: Is the proto-peer risk prone?

YES

Decision tree goes on to a fourth set of proto-peer's questions:

P-p: Is there a high capability differential between the hegemon and the proto-peer?

YES

Proto-peer changes strategy toward hegemon to 3 (alliance), leading to a current interaction of strategies: 2,3. The game now goes back to the hegemon, to evaluate whether the hegemon will change its own strategy as a result of a new strategy by the proto-peer. Hegemon goes back to the same decision tree choices but now fed with different information and with different assessments.

Heg: . . . [RESULT: continue playing as if starting point is 2,3]

****

H: YES, YES, LONG; P: YES, YES, YES, NO; (H: cont)

Heg: vulnerable?

YES

Decision tree goes on to a second set of questions:

Heg: are aims of proto-peer revisionist?

YES

Decision tree goes on to a third set of questions:

Heg: what is the time horizon for a challenge to appear?

LONG

Hegemon changes strategy toward proto-peer to 2 (co-opt), leading to a current interaction of strategies: 2,1. The game now goes on to the proto-peer, to evaluate whether the proto-peer will change its own strategy as a result of a new strategy by the hegemon.

P-p: Has the change in the hegemon's strategy placed high constraints on the proto-peer?

YES

Decision tree goes on to a second set of proto-peer's questions:

P-p: Is the proto-peer highly dissatisfied?

YES

Decision tree goes on to a third set of proto-peer's questions:

P-p: Is the proto-peer risk prone?

YES

Decision tree goes on to a fourth set of proto-peer's questions:

P-p: Is there a high capability differential between the hegemon and the proto-peer?

NO

Proto-peer changes strategy toward hegemon to 4 (conquest), leading to a current interaction of strategies: 2,4. The game now goes back to the hegemon, to evaluate whether the hegemon will change its own strategy as a result of a new strategy by the proto-peer. Hegemon goes back to the same decision tree choices but now fed with different information and with different assessments.

Heg: . . . [RESULT: continue playing as if starting point is 2,4]

****

H: YES, YES, SHORT, NO; P: NO

Heg: vulnerable?

YES

Decision tree goes on to a second set of questions:

Heg: are aims of proto-peer revisionist?

YES

Decision tree goes on to a third set of questions:

Heg: what is the time horizon for a challenge to appear?

SHORT

Decision tree goes on to a fourth set of questions:

Heg: is the threat severe?

NO

Hegemon changes strategy toward proto-peer to 3 (constrain), leading to a current interaction of strategies: 3,1. The game now goes on to the proto-peer, to evaluate whether the proto-peer will change its own strategy as a result of a new strategy by the hegemon.

P-p: Has the change in the hegemon's strategy placed high constraints on the proto-peer?

NO

Decision tree stops. Game remains at 3,1 (no need to go to hegemon response because no change in strategy by proto-peer)

RESULT: 3,1 (unstable)

{**Comment:** this result seems unstable in the long run, as it posits a hostile strategy by the hegemon but a nonthreatening strategy by the proto-peer; eventually, either the proto-peer will change strategies— escalate—or the hegemon will de-escalate. As hegemon and proto-peer re-evaluate, at least one is bound to make a change in strategies.}

****

H: YES, YES, SHORT, NO; P: YES, NO

Heg: vulnerable?

YES

Decision tree goes on to a second set of questions:

Heg: are aims of proto-peer revisionist?

YES

Decision tree goes on to a third set of questions:

Heg: what is the time horizon for a challenge to appear?

SHORT

Decision tree goes on to a fourth set of questions:

Heg: is the threat severe?

NO

Hegemon changes strategy toward proto-peer to 3 (constrain), leading to a current interaction of strategies: 3,1. The game now goes on to the proto-peer, to evaluate whether the proto-peer will change its own strategy as a result of a new strategy by the hegemon.

P-p: Has the change in the hegemon's strategy placed high constraints on the proto-peer?

YES

Decision tree goes on to a second set of questions:

P-p: Is the proto-peer highly dissatisfied?

NO

Decision tree stops. Game remains at 3,1 (no need to go to hegemon response because no change in strategy by proto-peer)

RESULT: 3,1 (unstable)

{**Comment:** this result seems unstable in the long run, as it posits a hostile strategy by the hegemon but a nonthreatening strategy by the proto-peer; eventually, either the proto-peer will change strategies—escalate—or the hegemon will de-escalate. As hegemon and proto-peer re-evaluate, at least one is bound to make a change in strategies.}

****

H: YES, YES, SHORT, NO; P: YES, YES, NO; (H: cont)

Heg: vulnerable?

YES

Decision tree goes on to a second set of questions:

Heg: are aims of proto-peer revisionist?

YES

Decision tree goes on to a third set of questions:

Heg: what is the time horizon for a challenge to appear?

SHORT

Decision tree goes on to a fourth set of questions:

Heg: is the threat severe?

NO

Hegemon changes strategy toward proto-peer to 3 (constrain), leading to a current interaction of strategies: 3,1. The game now goes on to the proto-peer, to evaluate whether the proto-peer will change its own strategy as a result of a new strategy by the hegemon.

P-p: Has the change in the hegemon's strategy placed high constraints on the proto-peer?

YES

Decision tree goes on to a second set of questions:

P-p: Is the proto-peer highly dissatisfied?

YES

Decision tree goes on to a third set of questions:

P-p: Is the proto-peer risk prone?

NO

Proto-peer changes strategy toward hegemon to 2 (revolution), leading to a current interaction of strategies: 3,2. The game now goes back to the hegemon, to evaluate whether the hegemon will change its own strategy as a result of a new strategy by the proto-peer. Hegemon goes back to the same decision tree choices but now fed with different information and with different assessments.

Heg: . . . [RESULT: continue playing as if starting point is 3,2]

****

H: YES, YES, SHORT, NO; P: YES, YES, YES, YES; (H: cont)

Heg: vulnerable?

YES

Decision tree goes on to a second set of questions:

Heg: are aims of proto-peer revisionist?

YES

Decision tree goes on to a third set of questions:

Heg: what is the time horizon for a challenge to appear?

SHORT

Decision tree goes on to a fourth set of questions:

Heg: is the threat severe?

NO

Hegemon changes strategy toward proto-peer to 3 (constrain), leading to a current interaction of strategies: 3,1. The game now goes on to the proto-peer, to evaluate whether the proto-peer will change its own strategy as a result of a new strategy by the hegemon.

P-p: Has the change in the hegemon's strategy placed high constraints on the proto-peer?

YES

Decision tree goes on to a second set of questions:

P-p: Is the proto-peer highly dissatisfied?

YES

Decision tree goes on to a third set of questions:

P-p: Is the proto-peer risk prone?

YES

Decision tree goes on to a fourth set of questions:

P-p: Is there a high capability differential between the hegemon and the proto-peer?

YES

Proto-peer changes strategy toward hegemon to 3 (alliance), leading to a current interaction of strategies: 3,3. The game now goes back to the hegemon, to evaluate whether the hegemon will change its own strategy as a result of a new strategy by the proto-peer. Hegemon goes back to the same decision tree choices but now fed with different information and with different assessments.

Heg: . . . [RESULT: continue playing as if starting point is 3,3]

****

H: YES, YES, SHORT, NO; P: YES, YES, YES, NO; (H: cont)

Heg: vulnerable?

YES

Decision tree goes on to a second set of questions:

Heg: are aims of proto-peer revisionist?

YES

Decision tree goes on to a third set of questions:

Heg: what is the time horizon for a challenge to appear?

SHORT

Decision tree goes on to a fourth set of questions:

Heg: is the threat severe?

NO

Hegemon changes strategy toward proto-peer to 3 (constrain), leading to a current interaction of strategies: 3,1. The game now goes on to the proto-peer, to evaluate whether the proto-peer will change its own strategy as a result of a new strategy by the hegemon.

P-p: Has the change in the hegemon's strategy placed high constraints on the proto-peer?

YES

Decision tree goes on to a second set of questions:

P-p: Is the proto-peer highly dissatisfied?

YES

Decision tree goes on to a third set of questions:

P-p: Is the proto-peer risk prone?

YES

Decision tree goes on to a fourth set of questions:

P-p: Is there a high capability differential between the hegemon and the proto-peer?

NO

Proto-peer changes strategy toward hegemon to 4 (conquest), leading to a current interaction of strategies: 3,4. The game now goes back to the hegemon, to evaluate whether the hegemon will change its own strategy as a result of a new strategy by the proto-peer. Hegemon goes back to the same decision tree choices but now fed with different information and with different assessments.

Heg: . . . [RESULT: continue playing as if starting point is 3,4]

****

H: YES, YES, SHORT, YES; P: NO

Heg: vulnerable?

YES

Decision tree goes on to a second set of questions:

Heg: are aims of proto-peer revisionist?

YES

Decision tree goes on to a third set of questions:

Heg: what is the time horizon for a challenge to appear?

SHORT

Decision tree goes on to a fourth set of questions:

Heg: is the threat severe?

YES

Hegemon changes strategy toward proto-peer to 4 (compete), leading to a current interaction of strategies: 4,1. The game now goes on to the proto-peer, to evaluate whether the proto-peer will change its own strategy as a result of a new strategy by the hegemon.

P-p: Has the change in the hegemon's strategy placed high constraints on the proto-peer?

NO

Decision tree stops. Game remains at 4,1 (no need to go to hegemon response because no change in strategy by proto-peer)

RESULT: 4,1 (unstable)

{**Comment:** this result seems unstable in the long run, as it posits a hostile strategy by the hegemon but a nonthreatening strategy by the proto-peer; eventually, either the proto-peer will change strategies—escalate—or the hegemon will de-escalate. As hegemon and proto-peer re-evaluate, at least one is bound to make a change in strategies.}

****

H: YES, YES, SHORT, YES; P: YES, NO

Heg: vulnerable?

> YES

> Decision tree goes on to a second set of questions:

Heg: are aims of proto-peer revisionist?

> YES

> Decision tree goes on to a third set of questions:

Heg: what is the time horizon for a challenge to appear?

> SHORT

> Decision tree goes on to a fourth set of questions:

Heg: is the threat severe?

> YES

> Hegemon changes strategy toward proto-peer to 4 (compete), leading to a current interaction of strategies: 4,1. The game now goes on to the proto-peer, to evaluate whether the proto-peer will change its own strategy as a result of a new strategy by the hegemon.

P-p: Has the change in the hegemon's strategy placed high constraints on the proto-peer?

> YES

> Decision tree goes on to a second set of questions:

P-p: Is the proto-peer highly dissatisfied?

NO

Decision tree stops. Game remains at 4,1 (no need to go to hegemon response because no change in strategy by proto-peer)

RESULT: 4,1 (unstable)

{**Comment:** this result seems unstable in the long run, as it posits a hostile strategy by the hegemon but a nonthreatening strategy by the proto-peer; eventually, either the proto-peer will change strategies—escalate—or the hegemon will de-escalate. As hegemon and proto-peer re-evaluate, at least one is bound to make a change in strategies.}

****

H: YES, YES, SHORT, YES; P: YES, YES, NO; (H: cont)

Heg: vulnerable?

YES

Decision tree goes on to a second set of questions:

Heg: are aims of proto-peer revisionist?

YES

Decision tree goes on to a third set of questions:

Heg: what is the time horizon for a challenge to appear?

SHORT

Decision tree goes on to a fourth set of questions:

Heg: is the threat severe?

YES

Hegemon changes strategy toward proto-peer to 4 (compete), leading to a current interaction of strategies: 4,1. The game now goes on to the proto-peer, to evaluate whether the proto-peer will change its own strategy as a result of a new strategy by the hegemon.

P-p: Has the change in the hegemon's strategy placed high constraints on the proto-peer?

YES

Decision tree goes on to a second set of questions:

P-p: Is the proto-peer highly dissatisfied?

YES

Decision tree goes on to a third set of questions:

P-p: Is the proto-peer risk prone?

NO

Proto-peer changes strategy toward hegemon to 2 (revolution), leading to a current interaction of strategies: 4,2. The game now goes back to the hegemon, to evaluate whether the hegemon will change its own strategy as a result of a new strategy by the proto-peer. Hegemon goes back to the same decision tree choices but now fed with different information and with different assessments.

Heg: . . . [RESULT: continue playing as if starting point is 4,2]

****

H: YES, YES, SHORT, YES; P: YES, YES, YES, YES; (H: cont)

Heg: vulnerable?

YES

Decision tree goes on to a second set of questions:

Heg: are aims of proto-peer revisionist?

YES

Decision tree goes on to a third set of questions:

Heg: what is the time horizon for a challenge to appear?

SHORT

Decision tree goes on to a fourth set of questions:

Heg: is the threat severe?

YES

Hegemon changes strategy toward proto-peer to 4 (compete), leading to a current interaction of strategies: 4,1. The game now goes on to the proto-peer, to evaluate whether the proto-peer will change its own strategy as a result of a new strategy by the hegemon.

P-p: Has the change in the hegemon's strategy placed high constraints on the proto-peer?

YES

Decision tree goes on to a second set of questions:

P-p: Is the proto-peer highly dissatisfied?

YES

Decision tree goes on to a third set of questions:

P-p: Is the proto-peer risk prone?

YES

Decision tree goes on to a fourth set of questions:

P-p: Is there a high capability differential between the hegemon and the proto-peer?

YES

Proto-peer changes strategy toward hegemon to 3 (alliance), leading to a current interaction of strategies: 4,3. The game now goes back to the hegemon, to evaluate whether the hegemon will change its own strategy as a result of a new strategy by the proto-peer. Hegemon goes back to the same decision tree choices but now fed with different information and with different assessments.

Heg: . . . [RESULT: continue playing as if starting point is 4,3]

****

H: YES, YES, SHORT, YES; P: YES, YES, YES, NO; (H: cont)

Heg: vulnerable?

> YES

> Decision tree goes on to a second set of questions:

Heg: are aims of proto-peer revisionist?

> YES

> Decision tree goes on to a third set of questions:

Heg: what is the time horizon for a challenge to appear?

> SHORT

> Decision tree goes on to a fourth set of questions:

Heg: is the threat severe?

> YES

> Hegemon changes strategy toward proto-peer to 4 (compete), leading to a current interaction of strategies: 4,1. The game now goes on to the proto-peer, to evaluate whether the proto-peer will change its own strategy as a result of a new strategy by the hegemon.

P-p: Has the change in the hegemon's strategy placed high constraints on the proto-peer?

> YES

> Decision tree goes on to a second set of questions:

P-p: Is the proto-peer highly dissatisfied?

> YES

> Decision tree goes on to a third set of questions:

P-p: Is the proto-peer risk prone?

YES

Decision tree goes on to a fourth set of questions:

P-p: Is there a high capability differential between the hegemon and the proto-peer?

NO

Proto-peer changes strategy toward hegemon to 4 (conquest), leading to a current interaction of strategies: 4,4. The game now goes back to the hegemon, to evaluate whether the hegemon will change its own strategy as a result of a new strategy by the proto-peer. Hegemon goes back to the same decision tree choices but now fed with different information and with different assessments.

Heg: . . . [RESULT: continue playing as if starting point is 4,4]

CODE FOR THE PROTOTYPE HEGEMON-PEER MODEL

PEERMODEL.H "HEADER FOR THE MODEL"

```
class Hegemon
{
private:
  int HVulnerable;
  int HAims_Revisionist;
  int HTime_Horizon;
  int HThreat_Severe;
  double* perceivedPower;
  float perceptError;

public:
  ~Hegemon() {
    delete[] perceivedPower;
  }
  void setEndTime(int endTime) {
    perceivedPower = new double[endTime+1];
  }
  void setPerceptError(float p) {perceptError = p;}

  int decide(int hstate, int cstate);
  void perceive(int cstate_change, int cstate, int hstate_change, int
      time, double power );
  void setHVulnerable(int i) {HVulnerable = i;}
  void setHAims_Revisionist(int i) {HAims_Revisionist = i;}
  void setHTime_Horizon(int i) {HTime_Horizon = i;}
  void setHThreat_Severe(int i) {HThreat_Severe = i;}
  int getVulnerable() { return HVulnerable;}
  int getAimsRevisionist() { return HAims_Revisionist;}
  int getTimeHorizon() { return HTime_Horizon;}
  int getThreatSevere() { return HThreat_Severe;}
```

```
};

class Challenger
{
private:
  int Cconstrained;
  int Cdissatisfied;
  int CriskProne;
  int CcapDifferential;
  double* perceivedPower;
  float perceptError;

public:
  ~Challenger() {delete[] perceivedPower;}
  void setEndTime(int endTime) {
    perceivedPower = new double[endTime+1];
  }
  void setPerceptError(float p) {perceptError = p;}
  int decide(int hstate, int cstate);
  void perceive(int hstate_change, int hstate, int cstate_change, int
       time, double power);
  void setCconstrained(int i) {Cconstrained = i;}
  void setCdissatisfied(int i) {Cdissatisfied = i;}
  void setCriskProne(int i) {CriskProne = i;}
//  void setCcapDifferential(int i) {CcapDifferential = i;}
  int getConstrained()  { return Cconstrained;}
  int getDissatisfied()  { return Cdissatisfied;}
  int getRiskProne()  { return CriskProne;}
  int getCapabilitydifferential()  { return CcapDifferential;}
};

class PeerModel
{
public:
  PeerModel() {
  }
  ~PeerModel() {
    delete [] challengerPower;
  }

  void setEndTime(int i) {
    endTime = i;
    challengerPower = new double[endTime+1];
    challenger.setEndTime(i);
```

```
  hegemon.setEndTime(i);
 }
 void setInitPower(double p) {challengerPower[0] = p;}
 void setBaseRate(float r) {baseRate = r;}
 void setHeffect (float* h) {
 int i;
  for(i=0;i<4; i++) Heffect[i] = h[i];
 }
 void setCeffect (float* c) {
  int i;
  for(i=0;i<4; i++) Ceffect[i] = c[i];
 }
 void setInitHstate(int i) { Hstate = i;}
 void setInitCstate(int i) {Cstate = i;}

 void run();
 double powerModel(double, int, int);

 int getHState() {return Hstate;}
 int getCState() {return Cstate;}
 Challenger* getChallenger()  {return &challenger;}
 Hegemon* getHegemon()  {return &hegemon;}


private:
  int endTime;
  int Hstate;
  int Cstate;

  double* challengerPower;
  float baseRate;   //these 3 vars create growth rate for Challenger power
  float Heffect[4];
  float Ceffect[4];

  Hegemon hegemon;
  Challenger challenger;
};
```

PEERMODEL.CPP "MODEL"
```
#include <math.h>

 long lrand48();
```

```
/*
 * Return a float between -range and +range.
 */

float RANDOM_WEIGHT (float range)
{
  return ( (float) (range * (rand()%1000 / 500.0)) - range );
}




double PeerModel::powerModel(double lastPower, int Hstate, int Cstate)
{
  double growthRate = baseRate + Heffect[Hstate] + Ceffect[Cstate];
  return lastPower * (1. + growthRate);
}


void PeerModel::run()
{
  int time;
  int lastCstate = Cstate;
  int lastHstate = Hstate;

  for(time=0; time<endTime; time++){
//cout << "run " << time << " " << Hstate << " " << Cstate << " " <<
challengerPower[time] << endl;

  int newHstate = hegemon.decide( Hstate, Cstate);
  challenger.perceive(newHstate-Hstate,newHstate,
    Cstate-lastCstate,  time, challengerPower[time]);
  lastHstate = Hstate;
  Hstate = newHstate;
  int newCstate = challenger.decide(Hstate, Cstate);
  hegemon.perceive(newCstate-Cstate,newCstate, Hstate-lastHstate,
    time, challengerPower[time]);
  lastCstate = Cstate;
  Cstate = newCstate;
  challengerPower[time+1] = powerModel(challengerPower[time],
    Hstate, Cstate);
  }

}
```

```
void Hegemon::perceive(int cstate_change, int cstate,
     int hstate_change, int time, double challengerPower)
{
//  HVulnerable unchanged
  perceivedPower[time] = challengerPower +
      RANDOM_WEIGHT(perceptError);
//cout << "hegemon " << challengerPower << " " << perceptError
     << " " << perceivedPower[time] << endl;

  if(cstate_change>0) HAims_Revisionist = 1;
//  if(cstate_change<0 & cstate < 3) HAims_Revisionist = 0;
  if(cstate_change<0 ) HAims_Revisionist = 0;
//  if(cstate_change == 0 & hstate_change>0 & cstate < 3)
        HAims_Revisionist = 0;
//  if(cstate_change == 0 & hstate_change<0 & cstate > 1)
        HAims_Revisionist = 1;
  if(cstate_change==0 & cstate==1) HAims_Revisionist = 0;
  if(time >= 1){
  float slope = perceivedPower[time] -perceivedPower[time-1];
  float timeWindow = (100.-perceivedPower[time])/slope;
     //hegemonPower = 100
  if(cstate <3 & timeWindow>20) HTime_Horizon = 0;   //long
  else if(cstate >2 & timeWindow>30) HTime_Horizon = 0;   //long
        else     HTime_Horizon = 1;

  if(cstate < 3 & timeWindow>10)  HThreat_Severe= 0;
  else if(cstate > 2 & timeWindow>20)  HThreat_Severe= 0;
        else     HThreat_Severe= 1;
  }
}


void Challenger::perceive(int hstate_change, int hstate, int
    cstate_change, int time, double challengerPower)
{
  perceivedPower[time] = challengerPower +
      RANDOM_WEIGHT(perceptError);
//cout << "challenger " << challengerPower << " " << perceptError
     << " " << perceivedPower[time] << endl;
  if(hstate_change>0) Cconstrained = 1;
  if(hstate_change<0 ) Cconstrained = 0;  //==0 -> unchanged
//  if(hstate_change<0 & hstate < 3) Cconstrained = 0;  //==0 ->
        unchanged
```

```
//   if(hstate_change == 0 & cstate_change>0 & hstate < 3)
        Cconstrained = 0;
//   if(hstate_change == 0 & cstate_change<0 & hstate > 1)
        Cconstrained = 1;
  if(hstate_change==0 & hstate==1) Cconstrained = 0;
// Cdissatisfied unchanged
// CriskProne unchanged
  if(hstate < 3 & perceivedPower[time] > 75.) CcapDifferential = 0;
  else if(hstate > 2 & perceivedPower[time] > 50) CcapDifferential = 0;
  else              CcapDifferential = 1;
}

int Hegemon:: decide (int hstate, int cstate)
{
  static int cooling = 0;
  if (HVulnerable == 0){
   if(cooling == 1) hstate = hstate -1;       //de-escalate
   else cooling = 1;        //remember you wanted to de-escalate next time
   if(hstate <1 ) hstate = 1; //can't go below conciliate
   return hstate;
   }
  cooling = 0;        // can't de-escalate next move
  if (HAims_Revisionist == 0) return cstate;    //aims== "no" => tit-for-tat
  if (HTime_Horizon == 0) {   // long
   hstate = hstate +1;        //tighten
   if(hstate >3 ) hstate = 3;  //can't go above in time horizon is long
   return hstate;
   }
  if (HThreat_Severe == 0) {
   hstate = hstate +2;        //escalate
   if(hstate >4 ) hstate = 4;  //can't go above Compete
   return hstate;
   }
  return 4;       //else Compete  (hstate+3 is always Compete)
}


int Challenger::decide(int hstate, int cstate)
{
  static int cooling = 0;
  if(Cconstrained == 0){
   if(cooling == 1) cstate = cstate -1;        //de-escalate
    else cooling = 1;        //can de-escalate next turn
   if(cstate <1 ) cstate = 1; //can't go below reform
```

```
 return cstate;
 }
 cooling = 0;        //can't de-escalate next move
 if(Cdissatisfied == 0) return cstate;   //dissatisfied = "no" => unchanged
 if(CriskProne == 0){
  cstate = cstate +1;       //not risk prone -> moderated response
  if(cstate >4 ) cstate = 4;  //can't go above Conquest
  if(CcapDifferential == 1 & cstate >3 ) cstate = 3;
  return cstate;
 }
 if(CcapDifferential == 1){  //high capability differential
  cstate = cstate +2;       //escalate
  if(cstate >3 ) cstate = 3;  //can't go above 3 if high cap differential
  return cstate;
 }
 return 4;      //else Conquest
}
```

**THE FOLLOWING CONNECTS THE MODEL TO THE ANALYTIC
ENVIRONMENT**
```
#include <math.h>
#include <stdlib.h>
#include "/usr/local/CARs/Lib/model.h"

#include "peerModel.h"
#include <string.h>

// For Windows NT Visual C++
#include <stdio.h>

#include "peerModel.cpp"

void run(expSpec* spec, expResult* result)
{
  srand(9876543);
  int num1 = 0;
  int num2 = 0;
  int num3 = 0;
  int num4 = 0;
  float percent1 = 0.;
  float percent2 = 0.;
  float percent3 = 0.;
  float percent4 = 0.;
```

```
float Heffect[4], Ceffect[4];

int index = 0;
int i;

int endTime = spec->getIntSpec(index++);
int initHstate = spec->getIntSpec(index++);
int initCstate = spec->getIntSpec(index++);
int hegInput = spec->getIntSpec(index++);
int compInput = spec->getIntSpec(index++);
float hPerceptError = spec->getFloatSpec(index++);
float cPerceptError = spec->getFloatSpec(index++);
double initPower = spec->getDoubleSpec(index++);
float baseRate = spec->getFloatSpec(index++);
for(i=0;i<4;i++) Heffect[i] = spec->getFloatSpec(index++);
for(i=0;i<4;i++) Ceffect[i] = spec->getFloatSpec(index++);
int nreps = spec->getIntSpec(index++);

//cout << endl << hegInput << " " << compInput << endl;

int hegThreat = 0;
int hegTimeHor = 0;
int hegAimsRev = 0;
int hegVuln = 0;
int compRiskProne = 0;
int compDiss = 0;
int compConstrain = 0;

if(hegInput == 1){        // "NYN"
   hegVuln = 0;
   hegTimeHor = 0;
   hegThreat = 0;
}
if(hegInput == 2){        // "NYY"
   hegVuln = 0;
   hegTimeHor = 0;
   hegThreat = 1;
}
if(hegInput == 3){        // "YNN"
   hegVuln = 1;
   hegTimeHor = 1;
   hegThreat = 0;
}
if(hegInput == 4){        // "YNY"
```

```
        hegVuln = 1;
        hegTimeHor = 1;
        hegThreat = 1;
    }
    if(hegInput == 5){        // "YYN"
        hegVuln = 1;
        hegTimeHor = 0;
        hegThreat = 0;
    }
    if(hegInput == 6){        // "YYY"
        hegVuln = 1;
        hegTimeHor = 0;
        hegThreat = 1;
    }

//      cout << "Hegemon: " << hegVuln << " " << hegAimsRev << " "
//            << hegTimeHor << " " << hegThreat << endl;


    if(compInput == 1){        // "NNN"
        compConstrain = 0;
        compDiss = 0;
        compRiskProne = 0;
    }
    if(compInput == 2){        // "NNY"
        compConstrain = 0;
        compDiss = 0;
        compRiskProne = 1;
    }
    if(compInput == 3){        // "NYN"
        compConstrain = 0;
        compDiss = 1;
        compRiskProne = 0;
    }
    if(compInput == 4){        // "NYY"
        compConstrain = 0;
        compDiss = 1;
        compRiskProne = 1;
    }
    if(compInput == 5){        // "YNN"
        compConstrain = 1;
        compDiss = 0;
        compRiskProne = 0;
    }
```

```
if(compInput == 6){        // "YNY"
   compConstrain = 1;
   compDiss = 0;
   compRiskProne = 1;
}
if(compInput == 7){        // "YYN"
   compConstrain = 1;
   compDiss = 1;
   compRiskProne = 0;
}
if(compInput == 8){        // "YYY"
   compConstrain = 1;
   compDiss = 1;
   compRiskProne = 1;
}

hegAimsRev = compDiss;

int hstate =  0;
int cstate = 0;
int vuln = 0;
int aims = 0;
int timeHor = 0;
int threatSev = 0;
int constrain = 0;
int dissat = 0;
int riskPr = 0;
int capDiff = 0;

num1 = num2 = num3 = num4 = 0;

for (i = 0; i<nreps; i++){
   PeerModel* peer_model = new PeerModel;
   Hegemon* hegemon = peer_model->getHegemon();
   Challenger* challenger = peer_model->getChallenger();

   peer_model->setEndTime(endTime);
   peer_model->setInitHstate(initHstate);
   peer_model->setInitCstate(initCstate);

   hegemon->setHVulnerable(hegVuln);
   hegemon->setHAims_Revisionist(hegAimsRev);
   hegemon->setHTime_Horizon(hegTimeHor);
   hegemon->setHThreat_Severe(hegThreat);
```

```
    challenger->setCconstrained(compConstrain);
    challenger->setCdissatisfied(compDiss);
    challenger->setCriskProne(compRiskProne);

    peer_model->setHeffect(Heffect);
    peer_model->setCeffect(Ceffect);

    hegemon->setPerceptError(hPerceptError);
    challenger->setPerceptError(cPerceptError);
    peer_model->setInitPower(initPower);
    peer_model->setBaseRate(baseRate);

    peer_model->run();

    hstate += peer_model->getHState();
    cstate += peer_model->getCState();
    vuln += hegemon->getVulnerable();
    aims += hegemon->getAimsRevisionist();
    timeHor += hegemon->getTimeHorizon();
    threatSev += hegemon->getThreatSevere();
    constrain += challenger->getConstrained();
    dissat += challenger->getDissatisfied();
    riskPr += challenger->getRiskProne();
    capDiff += challenger->getCapabilitydifferential();

    if(peer_model->getCState() == 1) num1++;
    if(peer_model->getCState() == 2) num2++;
    if(peer_model->getCState() == 3) num3++;
    if(peer_model->getCState() == 4) num4++;

    delete peer_model;
}

float fhstate    = hstate ;
float fcstate    = cstate;
float fvuln      = vuln;
float faims      = aims;
float ftimeHor   = timeHor;
float fthreatSev = threatSev;
float fconstrain = constrain;
float fdissat    = dissat;
float friskPr    = riskPr;
float fcapDiff   = capDiff;
```

```
percent1 = num1;
percent2 = num2;
percent3 = num3;
percent4 = num4;
percent1 = percent1/nreps;
percent2 = percent2/nreps;
percent3 = percent3/nreps;
percent4 = percent4/nreps;

index = 0;
result->setResult(index++,fhstate /nreps );
result->setResult(index++,fcstate/nreps );
result->setResult(index++,fvuln/nreps );
result->setResult(index++,faims/nreps );
result->setResult(index++,ftimeHor/nreps );
result->setResult(index++,fthreatSev/nreps );
result->setResult(index++,fconstrain/nreps );
result->setResult(index++,fdissat/nreps );
result->setResult(index++,friskPr/nreps );
result->setResult(index++,fcapDiff/nreps );
result->setResult(index++,percent1 );
result->setResult(index++,percent2 );
result->setResult(index++,percent3 );
result->setResult(index++,percent4 );

//cout << " result: " << peer_model->getHState() << " "
//    << peer_model->getCState() << endl;

}
```

THE DEMOCRATIC PEACE IDEA

One of the major tenets of U.S. foreign policy is the encouragement and support of democratization in the world. At the core of this argument is a national security objective of a less war-prone world. The linkage between a more peaceful world and more states with democratic political systems is the belief that democratic states are unlikely to fight wars against each other—what is often called the "democratic peace" proposition. One implication of the democratic peace is that the United States need not be concerned—or, at least, be less concerned—about potential proto-peers and peers that are democratic because such states will not pose a meaningful threat. In other words, if the democratic peace proposition is true, the competitive intent is lacking and a peer will not transform into a peer competitor.

While it has been true historically that democracies have refrained from waging war against each other, the relevance of the democratic peace for intelligence assessment concerning the rise of a peer competitor is less clear. This appendix reviews the literature concerning the three variants of the democratic peace proposition—the institutional, normative, and interdependence strands—and provides several reasons for caution regarding the use of democratic peace in the peer competitor context.

THE DEMOCRATIC PEACE PROPOSITION

The democratic peace proposition is perhaps the most widely accepted thesis among international relations theorists today. An immense body of literature in the field has been devoted to exploring the proposition[1] and, though there is a vocal dissenting minority, the consensus view is summed up in the remark that the "absence of war between democratic states comes as close as anything we have to an empirical law in international relations."[2] Although the idea is an old one, dating back to Immanuel Kant's writings in the 18th century, the explosion of scholarly interest in the topic has taken place since 1990.

The primary claim of democratic peace proponents is that democratic states do not wage war against each other, although a number of scholars have modified the claim to the proposition that "democracies are *less likely* to fight wars with each other."[3] The democratic peace also includes a handful of other claims, such as:

- Democracies tend to prevail in wars they fight with nondemocracies.[4]

- In wars they initiate, democracies suffer fewer casualties and fight shorter wars than nondemocratic states.[5]

- Democratic states locked in disputes with each other choose more peaceful means of resolution than other pairings of states.[6]

---

[1]For an evaluation of the current state of the field, see James Lee Ray, "Does Democracy Cause Peace?" *Annual Review of Political Science*, 1 (1998), pp. 27–46.

[2]Jack S. Levy, "The Causes of War: A Review of Theories and Evidence," in Philip E. Tetlock, Jo L. Husbands, Robert Jervis, Paul C. Stern, and Charles Tilly (eds.), *Behavior, Society, and Nuclear War*, Vol. 1, New York: Oxford University Press, 1989, p. 270.

[3]David A. Lake, "Powerful Pacifists: Democratic States and War," *American Political Science Review*, 86:1 (March 1992), p. 32 (emphasis added).

[4]David Lake, "Powerful Pacifists"; Dan Reiter and Allan C. Stam III, "Democracy, War Initiation, and Victory," *American Political Science Review*, 92:2 (June 1998), pp. 377–389.

[5]D. Scott Bennett and Allan C. Stam, "The Duration of Interstate Wars, 1816–1985," *American Political Science Review*, 90:2 (June 1996), pp. 239–257; Randolph M. Siverson, "Democracies and War Participation: In Defense of the Institutional Constraints Argument," *European Journal of International Relations*, 1 (December 1995), pp. 481–490.

[6]William J. Dixon, "Democracy and the Peaceful Settlement of International Conflict," *American Political Science Review*, 88:1 (March 1994), pp. 14–32; Michael Mousseau, "Democracy and Compromise in Militarized Interstate Conflicts, 1816–1992," *Journal of Conflict Resolution*, 42:2 (April 1998), pp. 210–230.

- Democratic great powers do not initiate preventive wars.[7]

Explanations of the democratic peace typically fall into one—or a combination of—three main categories:

- Democratic *institutions* place constraints on the ability of leaders to fight other democracies, or simply make them reluctant to choose war;

- *Norms* shared by democratic states cause them to view each other as pacific and unthreatening; and

- Democracy tends to foster *economic interdependence*, which reduces the likelihood of war.

Institutional Arguments

As illustrated in Figure C.1, democratic institutions are believed to cause peace in one of two ways. The most common argument is that the constitutional and legal restraints on executive action in democratic states—as well as the existence of free public debate—are a bulwark against peace for several reasons.[8] They give democracies sufficient time to work through disagreements peacefully, democracies are unlikely to fear that other democracies will initiate a surprise attack, and, in general, leaders are limited in their ability to independently launch wars against other democracies.

A more recent institutional argument focuses on the desire of democratic elites to be reelected.[9] Democratic leaders are primarily concerned about retaining office, and they are especially concerned about policy failure. Consequently, they fight harder and are more cautious: They try harder to win wars by spending more resources, and they only engage in fights they anticipate winning. Furthermore,

---

[7] Randall Schweller, "Domestic Structure and Preventive War: Are Democracies More Pacific?" *World Politics,* 44:2 (January 1992), pp. 235–269.

[8] John M. Owen, "How Liberalism Produces Democratic Peace," *International Security,* 19:2 (Fall 1994), pp. 87–125.

[9] Bruce Bueno de Mesquita, James D. Morrow, Randolph M. Siverson, and Alastair Smith, "An Institutional Explanation of the Democratic Peace," *American Political Science Review,* 93:4 (December 1999), pp. 791–807.

RAND*MR1346-C.1*

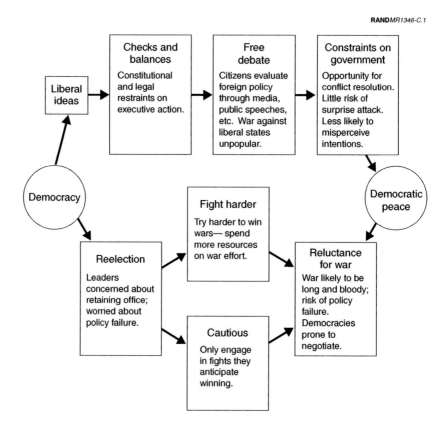

Figure C.1—Institutions and Democratic Peace

since democratic states contemplating war are likely to try harder, war is likely to be long and bloody and there is a greater risk of policy failure. Hence, democratic states are prone to negotiate with each other, rather than fight.

Normative Arguments

According to normative arguments, democracies believe that other democracies are reasonable, predictable, and trustworthy, as Figure C.2 highlights. Consequently, they will be disinclined to fight other democracies because they perceive that their intentions will always be pacific. In other words, democracies establish an atmosphere of "live and let live" with each other that results in a fundamental sense of stability.[10]

Interdependence Arguments

Democratic states have free-market economies, and, since they are better able to offer credible commitments regarding the terms of trade and capital flows than authoritarian states, they are more inclined to trade with one another.[11] As Figure C.3 exemplifies, interdependence promotes peace by increasing contacts among democracies and contributing to mutual understanding. Trade helps create transnational ties that encourage accommodation rather than conflict. Furthermore, trade is mutually beneficial to its participants, and war may negatively affect a country's economy because it could potentially cut off critical imports or exports. Finally, trade tends to decrease the benefits of conquest. Thus, the potential loss of trade decreases the willingness of both sides to fight.

RAND*MR1346-C.2*

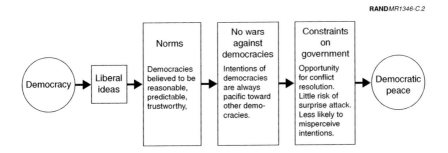

Figure C.2—Norms and Democratic Peace

---

[10]Zeev Maoz and Bruce M. Russett, "Normative and Structural Causes of Democratic Peace, 1946–1986," *American Political Science Review*, 87:3 (September 1993), pp. 624–638.

[11]John R. Oneal and Bruce M. Russett, "The Classical Liberals Were Right: Democracy, Interdependence, and Conflict, 1950–1985," *International Studies Quarterly*, 41:2 (June 1997), pp. 267–294.

RAND*MR1346-C.3*

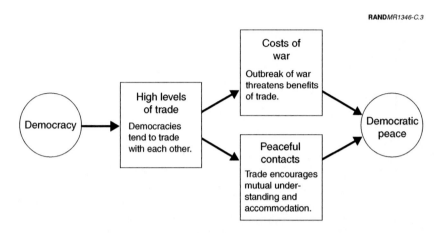

Figure C.3—Interdependence and Democratic Peace

CAVEATS

Many democratic peace proponents have been careful with their wording in noting that democracies are *less likely* to fight each other. This is, of course, a probabilistic—not a deterministic—statement. War may be unlikely between democracies, but it is nonetheless possible. Since security rests on being prepared for all types of situations, the probabilistic statement removes a good deal of the relevance of the democratic peace proposition in the context of the work on a peer competitor.

For defense intelligence purposes, the following conditions are important caveats to the democratic peace proposition when competition is with democratic peer competitors. In an overall sense, these conditions demonstrate that the prudent course of action for the United States is that it needs to retain concern about the rise of democratic peer competitors, even if the probability of large-scale war between democratic states has historically been very low. After all, during the Cold War there was hostile competition between the United States and the Soviet Union, though direct military conflict between the two was averted. A short list includes six conditions (each examined in greater detail below):

- Democratic states are not immune from security competition and wars with nondemocracies, both of which could bring them into conflict with the United States.

- Democratizing states may be more war-prone.

- Perceptions of other democracies as peaceful and friendly can change if there is substantial security or economic competition.

- Democracies may resort to proxy wars or covert action, rather than direct conflict.

- There have been numerous periods of democratic reversals in history and there may be some in the future.

- Democratic peace may be an example of high correlation rather than causation, making it of questionable utility for intelligence purposes.

Security Competition

While democratic peace arguments have drawn attention to the statistical fact that democracies have historically not been involved in wars with other democracies, democratic states have engaged in hostile competition with each other. In general, changes in the relative capabilities of rising powers tend to trigger changes in their behavior. Typically, they will want more influence commensurate with their increased power, and they may be less willing to back down during disputes.[12] Consequently, proto-peers that become increasingly powerful relative to the United States—regardless of regime type—are likely to push for increased influence in areas that they consider strategically important. This might take one of two forms.

First, security competition might lead the United States and a democratic proto-peer to clash over influence in a specific region or coun-

---

[12]With perhaps a few exceptions, the historical record shows that rising powers generally seek to expand their influence. For instance, an increasingly powerful United States in the latter half of the 19th century implemented the expansionist policy of "Manifest Destiny," followed by increasing interventionism in Latin America, the Pacific, and East Asia. Great Britain, Weimar and Nazi Germany, Czarist Russia, and the Soviet Union followed this somewhat general pattern: Increases in state power led to an expansion of political interests abroad. Zakaria, *From Wealth to Power.*

try. This would not *ipso facto* lead to war. Given that the United States has strong interest and is involved in the security realm in much of the world, it would hardly be surprising to have security competition in areas where there was a conflict of interest. Second, as many democratic peace proponents freely admit, democracies have fought numerous wars with—and used violence against—authoritarian states.[13] They have been aggressors, pursued imperialistic policies, and built empires; in sum, they are not immune from policies of subjugation and belligerence. It is conceivable that the United States might consider coming to the aid of a nondemocratic state that has been either attacked or intimidated by a rising democratic proto-peer. If such aid were to be extended in areas that were of strategic importance to the United States, the probability of conflict would be greater.

Democratization

Although this is not an argument accepted universally among democratic peace proponents, some scholars claim that states that are in the process of democratization—and that have not become established, consolidated democracies—tend to be more warlike.[14] Indeed, democratization can be an extremely rocky and tenuous transitional period, and, depending on the definition of a transitional period, there is evidence to suggest that democratizing states are more inclined to fight wars than are states that do not undergo regime change. Several factors seem to affect the probability of war during transition:

- Democratization leads to the establishment of a number of politically significant groups with diverse and sometimes conflicting platforms.

- Threatened elites have an impetus to mobilize allies among the mass population, sometimes along nationalist lines.

- State authority in general is weak and unstable.

---

[13]Zeev Maoz and Nasrin Abdolali, "Regime Types and International Conflict, 1816–1976," *Journal of Conflict Resolution*, 33:1 (March 1989), pp. 3–35.

[14]"Democratization" refers to the process where states have undergone a regime change in a democratic direction.

Specifically, the danger of war increases when elites attempt to retain or increase mass support by utilizing nationalist or populist themes during the democratization process—and trigger mass nationalism and elite logrolling.[15] Furthermore, this transition period can also be destabilized by civil war, which often breaks out for many of the reasons listed above.[16]

Since the democratization process can be extremely unstable, and since states that are in this transition period may be more warlike and often suffer destabilizing and bloody civil wars, peers and proto-peers undergoing democratic transitions may be an especially worrisome problem for the United States. Democratization can be a fairly long process—perhaps occurring over several decades—and, even then, the creation of a consolidated democratic political system is by no means inevitable.

Changing Perceptions

Normative explanations of the democratic peace contend that democratic states externalize their domestic political norms of tolerance and compromise in their foreign relations with other democratic states. As two proponents note: "Political conflicts in democracies are resolved through compromise rather than through elimination of opponents. This norm allows for an atmosphere of 'live and let live' that results in a fundamental sense of stability at the

---

[15]Edward D. Mansfield and Jack Snyder, "Democratization and the Danger of War," *International Security*, 20:1 (Summer 1995), pp. 5–38; Edward D. Mansfield and Jack Snyder, "Democratization and War," *Foreign Affairs*, 74:2 (May/June 1995), pp. 79–97; Jack L. Snyder, *From Voting to Violence: Democratization and Nationalist Conflict*, New York: W. W. Norton, 2000; and Michael D. Ward and Kristian S. Gleditsch, "Democratizing for Peace," *American Political Science Review*, 92:1 (March 1998), pp. 51–61.

[16]A number of authors have posited that the democratization and war argument is either overstated or that regime change and war involvement are independent of one another. See, for example, William R. Thompson and Richard Tucker, "A Tale of Two Democratic Peace Critiques," *Journal of Conflict Resolution*, 41:3 (June 1997), pp. 428–454; Reinhard Wolf, Erich Weede, Andrew J. Enterline, and Edward D. Mansfield and Jack Snyder, "Correspondence: Democratization and the Danger of War," *International Security*, 20:4 (Spring 1996), pp. 176–207.

personal, communal, and national level."[17]   Moreover, borrowing from Immanuel Kant's Second Definitive Article, democratic peace arguments explain that international law entreats democratic states to harbor mutual respect for each other.[18]   Kant notes: "As culture grows and men gradually move towards greater agreement over their principles, they lead to mutual understanding and peace."[19]

However, recent examples demonstrate that perceptions of other democracies can change rapidly and decisively.[20]   For instance, economic competition between the United States and Japan in the late 1980s and early 1990s led to significant tension between them and led to public opinion in both countries shifting to view the other as a competitor. The point here is significant. While democratic states have frequently considered other democratic states unthreatening, norms of respect and perceptions of friendliness can change when states are faced with substantial security—or even economic—competition. This is an important finding for assessing potential peer competitors because it suggests that hostile competition between the United States and another democratic great power is not a remote possibility; democratic norms and perceptions are not infallible.

Covert Action and Proxy Wars

Democratic peace arguments focus predominantly on the unlikelihood of interstate war between democracies—where war is defined

---

[17]Zeev Maoz and Bruce Russett, "Normative and Structural Causes of Democratic Peace, 1946–1986," *American Political Science Review*, 87:3 (September 1993), pp. 624–638.

[18]Michael W. Doyle, "Liberalism and World Politics," *American Political Science Review*, 80:4 (December 1996), pp. 1151–1169.

[19]Immanuel Kant, *Kant's Political Writings*, Hans Reiss (ed.), H.B. Nisbet (trans.), Cambridge: Cambridge University Press, 1970, p. 114.

[20]For a historical account of changing perceptions of democracies, see Ido Oren, "The Subjectivity of the 'Democratic' Peace: Changing U.S. Perceptions of Imperial Germany," *International Security*, 20:2 (Fall 1995), pp. 147–184; Joanne Gowa, "Democratic States and International Disputes," *International Organization*, 49:3 (Summer 1995), pp. 511–522; and Joanne Gowa, *Ballots and Bullets: The Elusive Democratic Peace*, Princeton, NJ: Princeton University Press, 1999.

as a minimum of 1,000 battle deaths.[21] One problem with this definition, however, is that it ignores conflict at lower levels of violence, such as covert action and low levels of armed conflict, against democratic and democratizing states.[22] Such examples do show that democratic states are willing to use force against other democracies. This has an important implication *vis-à-vis* future proto-peers and peers because it suggests that United States competitors might engage in covert action, rather than direct conflict.

Another related problem with the democratic peace is that it fails to note the possibility of proxy wars. In a very real sense, the Cold War—the preeminent contemporary version of hostile peer competition—was fought *en masse* as a series of covert operations and proxy wars.[23] Indeed, the future competition between the United States and a potential peer competitor would not *ipso facto* have to lead to direct military confrontation. Instead, conflict could occur on the periphery in third states.

Democratic Reversals

The number of democratic states has increased exponentially over the course of the 20th century, but the upswing has not been constant. Instead, it should come as no surprise that democracy has progressed in fits and starts, with as many as 70 instances when democratic states have suffered reversals.[24] Democracy, like history, is not unidirectional. As Samuel Huntington notes, the first two waves of democratization (1828–1926 and 1943–1962) were followed by reverse waves (1922–1942 and 1958–1975).[25] There have been cases of democratic great powers that have suffered reversals. Twentieth century examples include Italy in the 1920s and Germany

---

[21]This benchmark is used by the Correlates of War database at the University of Michigan.

[22]Exceptions include David P. Forsythe, "Democracy, War, and Covert Action," *Journal of Peace Research*, 29:4 (1992), pp. 385–395.

[23]See, for example, John Lewis Gaddis, "The Long Peace: Elements of Stability in the Postwar International System," *International Security*, 10:4 (Spring 1986), pp. 99–142.

[24]Robert A. Dahl, *On Democracy*, New Haven, CT: Yale University Press, 2000, p. 145.

[25]Samuel P. Huntington, *The Third Wave: Democratization in the Late Twentieth Century*, Norman and London: University of Oklahoma Press, 1991.

and Japan in the 1930s. It is perhaps telling that each of these states subsequently went on an aggressive foreign spree.[26]

The fact that reversals do happen has implications for current debates concerning proto-peers and potential peer competitors to the United States. First, consolidated democratic great powers—states that have established the norms and practices of a strong and grounded civil society, a fully functioning political society, a rule of law that is upheld and respected, a state apparatus that respects, protects, and upholds the rights of citizens, and a market-oriented economic society—appear substantially *less likely* to suffer a democratic reversal.[27]   Of course, in the long term no country is ever completely immune from slipping into decline and eventually into authoritarianism. Yet the very fact that democracy has become firmly entrenched in the norms and practices of consolidated states—that it has become "the only game in town"—makes them *de facto* much less vulnerable to reversals.

Second, democratic states that have either begun to slip into decline or are perhaps still in the process of a transition are much more vulnerable to reversals. Indeed, Russia has a recent authoritarian past, and India suffered a democratic setback in the mid-1970s and has democratic institutions that are of questionable effectiveness.[28] Furthermore, as the German, Japanese, and Italian cases suggest, democratic reversals can lead to aggressive foreign excursions.

Causal Logic

While an impressive amount of statistical research has demonstrated that democratic states historically have refrained from waging war on each other, the causal explanations have been much more contentious. Opponents of the democratic peace idea contend that the

---

[26]Snyder and Mansfield, "Democratization and the Danger of War," pp. 30–31.

[27]For work on consolidated democracies see Juan J. Linz and Alfred C. Stepan, *Problems of Democratic Transition and Consolidation: Southern Europe, South America, and Post-Communist Europe,* Baltimore and London, John Hopkins University Press, 1996, pp. 3–15.

[28]Patrick Heller, "Degrees of Democracy: Some Comparative Lessons from India," *World Politics,* 52:4 (July 2000), pp. 484–519.

phenomenon may simply be a function of high correlation, rather than causation. Such arguments can be put into four groups.

First, if democratic institutions had a pacifying effect on leaders—through constitutional and legal restraints, free public debate, or the desire to be reelected—they would have peaceful relations with *all* states. Second, normative arguments have several deficiencies. As noted earlier, the view that democratic states externalize peaceful norms of behavior with other democracies is contradicted by the fact that they can still engage in security competition, utilize covert action, and change perceptions of other democracies as friendly depending on the context. Moreover, a number of wars between democracies were averted because of adverse distributions of military capabilities and concerns that other states would take advantage of the fight—not because of normative "live and let live" reasons.[29] Third, interdependence arguments in general are suspect because interdependence may very well help promote war, as well as peace. On the one hand, it may help cause peace by augmenting contacts among states and contributing to mutual understanding; on the other, it increases the occasion for conflicts that may promote resentment and even war.[30] Thus, interdependence may be an *effect* of peace—rather than a *cause* of it. Fourth, some scholars claim that statistical evidence suggests that only after 1945 did pairs of democracies become significantly less war-prone. However, peace between democracies during the post-1945 period may have been largely a function of alliance patterns caused by the Cold War, rather than democratic peace explanations.[31]

All of the above arguments continue to be hotly debated. Moreover, probably the most interesting development in the democratic peace area over the last two years has been the emergence of a causal, em-

---

[29]Christopher Layne, "Kant or Cant: The Myth of the Democratic Peace," *International Security*, 19:2 (Fall 1994), pp. 5–49.

[30]Katherine Barbieri, "Economic Interdependence: A Path to Peace or a Source of Interstate Conflict?" *Journal of Peace Research*, 33:1 (February 1996), pp. 29–49; Kenneth N. Waltz, "Structural Realism After the Cold War," *International Security*, 25:1 (Summer 2000), pp. 5–41.

[31]Henry S. Farber, "Polities and Peace," *International Security*, 20:2 (Fall 1995), pp. 123–146. Also see David E. Spiro, "The Insignificance of the Liberal Peace," *International Security*, 19:2 (Fall 1994), pp. 50–86. For an argument against this objection, see Thompson and Tucker, "A Tale of Two Democratic Peace Critiques."

pirically tested linkage between democracy and peace.[32] In short, the argument borrows from all three variants of the democratic peace school and posits that the crucial variable is the presence of a multitude of pacifying mechanisms in democracies that generally do not allow disputes to develop to a point of a crisis. If the disputes actually develop to such a level, then democracy has no independent effect on further escalation to a war, but the presence of the pacifying mechanisms on both sides generally prevents such an evolution. The logic explains why there have been a few isolated cases of democratic states waging war on each other, points out the critical juncture at which democratic political systems have a pacifying effect, and links the incidence of tensions, conflict, and war into one process. Subject to additional statistical testing, the proposition may be the proof needed for democratic peace proponents. However, even if true, the explanation remains probabilistic and does not eliminate the need for caution in U.S. assessments of proto-peers and peers. It is helpful to note the historical paucity of conflict between democracies and it is reassuring that consolidated democracies are less likely to wage war on each other, but it is a different matter to project the behavior of future democratic states based on the evidence presented so far.

---

[32]William Reed, "A Unified Statistical Model of Conflict Onset and Escalation," *American Journal of Political Science*, 44:1 (January 2000), pp. 84–93.

BIBLIOGRAPHY

Altfeld, Michael. "The Decision to Ally: A Theory and Test," *The Western Political Quarterly*, 37:4 (December 1984), pp. 523–544.

Ayres, Robert U. "On Forecasting Discontinuities," *Technological Forecasting and Social Change*, 65:1 (September 2000), pp. 81–97.

Bacevich, A. J. "Just War II: Morality and High-Technology," *The National Interest*, 45 (Fall 1996), pp. 37–47.

Bacevich, Andrew J. *The Pentomic Era: the US Army Between Korea and Vietnam*, Washington, D.C.: National Defense University Press, 1986.

Barbieri, Katherine. "Economic Interdependence: A Path to Peace or a Source of Interstate Conflict?" *Journal of Peace Research*, 33:1 (February 1996), pp. 29–49.

Barro, Robert J., *Determinants of Economic Growth: A Cross-Country Empirical Study*, Cambridge, MA: National Bureau of Economic Research, 1996.

Bennett, D. Scott, and Allan C. Stam. "The Duration of Interstate Wars, 1816–1985," *American Political Science Review*, 90:2 (June 1996), pp. 239–257.

Bercovitch, Jacob, and Gerald Schneider. "Who Mediates? The Political Economy of International Conflict Management," *Journal of Peace Research*, 37:2 (2000), pp. 145–165.

Biddle, Stephen. "The Past as Prologue: Assessing Theories of Future Warfare," *Security Studies*, 8:1 (Autumn 1998), pp. 1–74.

Birdsall, Nancy, and Richard Sabot. "Inequality as a Constraint on Growth in Latin America," in Mitchell A. Seligson and John T. Passé-Smith (eds.), *Development and Underdevelopment: The Political Economy of Global Inequality*, 2nd ed., Boulder, CO: Lynne Rienner Publishers, Inc., 1998.

Blank, Stephen. "Preparing for the Next War: Reflections on the Revolution in Military Affairs," *Strategic Review*, 24:2 (Spring 1996), pp. 17–25.

Bond, Brian, and Williamson Murray. "British Armed Forces, 1918–1939," in Allan R. Millett and Williamson Murray (eds.), *Military Effectiveness, Volume II*, Boston: Unwin Hyman, 1988.

Bremer, Stuart A. "Dangerous Dyads: Conditions Affecting the Likelihood of Interstate War: 1816–1965," *Journal of Conflict Resolution*, 36:2 (1992), pp. 309–341.

Brooks, Stephen G. "The Globalization of Production and the Changing Benefits of Conquest," *Journal of Conflict Resolution*, 43:5 (October 1999), pp. 646–670.

Bueno de Mesquita, Bruce, and David Lalman. *War and Reason: Domestic and International Imperatives*, New Haven, CT: Yale University Press, 1992.

Bueno de Mesquita, Bruce, James D. Morrow, Randolph M. Siverson, and Alastair Smith. "An Institutional Explanation of the Democratic Peace," *American Political Science Review*, 93:4 (December 1999), pp. 791–807.

Buzan, Barry. "'Change and Insecurity' Reconsidered," *Contemporary Security Policy*, 20:3 (December 1999), pp. 1–17.

Castillo, Jasen, Julia Lowell, Ashley J. Tellis, Jorge Muñoz, Benjamin Zycher. *Military Expenditures and Economic Growth*, Santa Monica, CA: RAND, MR-1112-A, 2001.

Cerf, Christopher, and Victor Navasky. *The Experts Speak*, New York: Villard, 1998.

Christensen, Thomas J. "Perceptions and Alliances in Europe, 1865–1940," *International Organization*, 51:1 (Winter 1997), pp. 65–97.

Cohen, Eliot. "A Revolution in Warfare," *Foreign Affairs*, 75:2 (March/April 1996), pp. 37–54.

Cortell, Andrew P., and James W. Davis, Jr. "How Do International Institutions Matter? The Domestic Impact of International Rules and Norms," *International Studies Quarterly*, 40:4 (December 1996), pp. 451–478.

Dahl, Robert A. *On Democracy*, New Haven, CT: Yale University Press, 2000.

DiCicco, Jonathan M., and Jack S. Levy. "Power Shifts and Problem Shifts: The Evolution of the Power Transition Research Program," *Journal of Conflict Resolution*, 43:6 (December 1999), pp. 675–704.

Diehl, Paul F. (ed.). *The Dynamics of Enduring Rivalries*, Urbana: University of Illinois Press, 1998.

Dixon, William J. "Democracy and the Peaceful Settlement of International Conflict," *American Political Science Review*, 88:1 (March 1994), pp. 14–32.

Doran, Charles F. "Why Forecasts Fail: The Limits and Potential of Forecasting in International Relations and Economics," *International Studies Review*, 1:2 (1999), pp. 11–41.

Doyle, Michael W. "Liberalism and World Politics," *American Political Science Review*, 80:4 (December 1996), pp. 1151–1169.

Easterly, William, and Stanley Fischer. "The Soviet Economic Decline," *World Bank Economic Review*, 9:3 (1995), pp. 341–371.

Farber, Henry S. "Polities and Peace," *International Security*, 20:2 (Fall 1995), pp. 123–146.

Forsythe, David P. "Democracy, War, and Covert Action," *Journal of Peace Research*, 29:4 (1992), pp. 385–395.

Franck, Raymond E., Jr. and Gregory G. Hildebrandt. "Competitive Aspects of the Contemporary Military-Technical Revolution: Potential Military Rivals to the U.S.," *Defense Analysis*, 12:2 (August 1996), pp. 239–258.

Friedman, Milton. *Capitalism and Freedom*, Chicago: University of Chicago Press, 1962.

Gaddis, John Lewis. "The Long Peace: Elements of Stability in the Postwar International System," *International Security*, 10:4 (Spring 1986), pp. 99–142.

Gautschi, Thomas. "History Effects in Social Dilemma Situations," *Rationality and Society*, 12:2 (May 2000), pp. 131–162.

Gilpin, Robert, *War and Change in World Politics*, Cambridge and New York: Cambridge University Press, 1981.

Goertz, Gary, and Paul F. Diehl. "The Initiation and Termination of Enduring Rivalries: The Impact of Political Shocks," *American Journal of Political Science*, 39:1 (February 1995), pp. 30–52.

Goldman, Emily O., and Richard B. Andres. "Systemic Effects of Military Innovation and Diffusion," *Security Studies*, 8:4 (Summer 1999), pp. 79–125.

Gowa, Joanne. *Ballots and Bullets: The Elusive Democratic Peace*, Princeton, NJ: Princeton University Press, 1999.

Gowa, Joanne. "Democratic States and International Disputes," *International Organization*, 49:3 (Summer 1995), pp. 511–522.

Grossman, Gene M., and Elhanan Helpman. *Innovation and Growth in the Global Economy*, Cambridge: MIT Press, 1991.

Heller, Patrick. "Degrees of Democracy: Some Comparative Lessons from India," *World Politics*, 52:4 (July 2000), pp. 484–519.

Hensel, Paul R. "An Evolutionary Approach to the Study of Interstate Rivalry," *Conflict Management and Peace Science*, 17:2 (Fall 1999), pp. 175–206.

Hudson, Valerie M. "Cultural Expectations of One's Own and Other Nations' Foreign Policy Action Templates," *Political Psychology*, 20:4 (December 1999), pp. 767–801.

Huntington, Samuel P. *The Third Wave: Democratization in the Late Twentieth Century*, Norman and London: University of Oklahoma Press, 1991.

Huth, Paul K. "Enduring Rivalries and Territorial Disputes, 1950–1990," *Conflict Management and Peace Science*, 15:1 (1996), pp. 7–41.

James, Patrick, "Structural Realism and the Causes of War," *Mershon International Studies Review*, 39 (1995), pp. 181–208.

Jervis, Robert, "Cooperation Under the Security Dilemma," *World Politics*, 30:2 (January 1978), pp. 167–214.

Kadera, Kelly M. "The Power-Conflict Story: A Synopsis," *Conflict Management and Peace Science*, 17:2 (Fall 1999), pp. 149–174.

Kammler, Hans. "Not for Security Only: The Demand for International Status and Defence Expenditure: An Introduction," *Defence and Peace Economics*, 8:1 (1997), pp. 1–18.

Kant, Immanuel. *Kant's Political Writings*, Hans Reiss (ed.), H.B. Nisbet (trans.), Cambridge: Cambridge University Press, 1970.

Kennedy, Paul M., *The Rise and Fall of the Great Powers: Economic Change and Military Conflict from 1500 to 2000*, New York: Random House, 1987.

Khalilzad, Zalmay, Abram N. Shulsky, Daniel Byman, Roger Cliff, David T. Orletsky, David A. Shlapak, and Ashley J. Tellis. *The United States and a Rising China*, Santa Monica, CA: RAND, 1999.

Kim, Woosang, and James D. Morrow. "When Do Power Shifts Lead to War?" *American Journal of Political Science*, 36:4 (November 1992), pp. 896–922.

Kowert, Paul A., and Margaret G. Hermann. "Who Takes Risks? Daring and Caution in Foreign Policy Making," *Journal of Conflict Resolution*, 41:5 (October 1997), pp. 611–637.

Krasner, Stephen D. *Sovereignty: Organized Hypocrisy*, Princeton, NJ: Princeton University Press, 1999.

Krepinevich, Andrew. "From Cavalry to Computer: The Pattern of Military Revolution," *The National Interest*, 37 (Fall 1994), pp. 30–42.

Kugler, Jacek, and Douglas Lemke (eds.). *Parity and War: Evaluations and Extensions of "The War Ledger,"* Ann Arbor, MI: University of Michigan Press, 1996.

Lake, David A. "Powerful Pacifists: Democratic States and War," *American Political Science Review*, 86:1 (March 1992), pp. 24–37.

Layne, Christopher. "Kant or Cant: The Myth of the Democratic Peace," *International Security*, 19:2 (Fall 1994), pp. 5–49.

Leng, Russell J. "When Will They Ever Learn: Coercive Bargaining in Recurrent Crises," *Journal of Conflict Resolution*, 27:3 (September 1983), pp. 379–419.

Levy, Jack S. "Alliance Formation and War Behavior: An Analysis of the Great Powers, 1495–1975," *Journal of Conflict Resolution*, 25:4 (December 1981), pp. 581–613.

Levy, Jack S. "The Causes of War: A Review of Theories and Evidence," in Philip E. Tetlock, Jo L. Husbands, Robert Jervis, Paul C. Stern, and Charles Tilly (eds.), *Behavior, Society, and Nuclear War*, Vol. 1, New York: Oxford University Press, 1989.

Liberman, Peter. *Does Conquest Pay? The Exploitation of Occupied Industrial Societies*, Princeton, NJ: Princeton University Press, 1996.

Linz, Juan J., and Alfred C. Stepan, *Problems of Democratic Transition and Consolidation: Southern Europe, South America, and Post-Communist Europe*, Baltimore and London, John Hopkins University Press, 1996.

Mandelbaum, Michael. "Is Major War Obsolete?" *Survival*, 40:4 (Winter 1998–1999), pp. 20–38.

Mansfield, Edward D., and Jack Snyder. "Democratization and the Danger of War," *International Security*, 20:1 (Summer 1995), pp. 5–38.

Mansfield, Edward D., and Jack Snyder. "Democratization and War," *Foreign Affairs*, 74:2 (May/June 1995), pp. 79–97.

Maoz, Zeev, and Nasrin Abdolali. "Regime Types and International Conflict, 1816–1976," *Journal of Conflict Resolution*, 33:1 (March 1989), pp. 3–35.

Maoz, Zeev, and Bruce M. Russett. "Normative and Structural Causes of Democratic Peace, 1946–1986," *American Political Science Review*, 87:3 (September 1993), pp. 624–638.

McDermott, Rose. *Risk-Taking in International Politics: Prospect Theory in American Foreign Policy*, Ann Arbor, MI: University of Michigan Press, 1998.

Meernik, James. "Force and Influence in International Crises," *Conflict Management and Peace Science*, 17:1 (1999), pp. 103–131.

Mor, Ben D., and Zeev Maoz. "Learning and the Evolution of Enduring International Rivalries: A Strategic Approach," *Conflict Management and Peace Science*, 17:1 (1999), pp. 1–48.

Morgan, Patrick. *Deterrence: A Conceptual Analysis*, 2nd ed., Beverly Hills: Sage, 1983.

Morrow, James. "Alliances and Asymmetry: An Alternative to the Capability Aggregation Model of Alliances," *American Journal of Political Science*, 35:4 (November 1991), pp. 904–933.

Morrow, James. "Arms Versus Allies: Trade-offs in the Search for Security," *International Organization*, 47:2 (Spring 1993), pp. 207–234.

Moul, William Brian. "Balances of Power and the Escalation to War of Serious Disputes Among the European Great Powers, 1815–1939: Some Evidence," *American Journal of Political Science*, 32:2 (May 1988), pp. 241–275.

Mousseau, Michael. "Democracy and Compromise in Militarized Interstate Conflicts, 1816–1992," *Journal of Conflict Resolution*, 42:2 (April 1998), pp. 210–230.

Mueller, John. *Retreat from Doomsday: The Obsolescence of Major War*, New York: Basic Books, 1989.

Murray, Williamson. "Armored Warfare: The British, French, and German Experiences," in Williamson Murray and Allan R. Millett (eds.), *Military Innovation in the Interwar Period*, Cambridge: Cambridge University Press, 1996.

Olson, Mancur. *Power and Prosperity: Outgrowing Communist and Capitalist Dictatorships*, New York: Basic Books, 2000.

Olson, Mancur. *The Rise and Decline of Nations: Economic Growth, Stagflation, and Social Rigidities*, New Haven: Yale University Press, 1982.

Olson, Mancur, Jr., and Richard Zeckhauser. "An Economic Theory of Alliances," *Review of Economics and Statistics*, 48:3 (August 1966), pp. 266–279.

Oneal, John R., and Bruce M. Russett. "The Classical Liberals Were Right: Democracy, Interdependence, and Conflict, 1950–1985," *International Studies Quarterly*, 41:2 (June 1997), pp. 267–294.

Oren, Ido. "The Subjectivity of the 'Democratic' Peace: Changing U.S. Perceptions of Imperial Germany," *International Security*, 20:2 (Fall 1995), pp. 147–184.

Organski, A.F.K. *World Politics*, New York: Alfred A. Knopf, 1958.

Organski, A.F.K., and Jacek Kugler. *The War Ledger*, Chicago: University of Chicago Press, 1980.

Owen, John M. "How Liberalism Produces Democratic Peace," *International Security*, 19:2 (Fall 1994), pp. 87–125.

Parker, Geoffrey. *The Military Revolution: Military Innovation and the Rise of the West, 1500–1800*, New York: Cambridge University Press, 1996.

Ray, James Lee. "Does Democracy Cause Peace?" *Annual Review of Political Science*, 1 (1998), pp. 27–46.

Reed, William. "A Unified Statistical Model of Conflict Onset and Escalation," *American Journal of Political Science*, 44:1 (January 2000), pp. 84–93.

Reiter, Dan, and Allan C. Stam III. "Democracy, War Initiation, and Victory," *American Political Science Review*, 92:2 (June 1998), pp. 377–389.

Richardson, Lewis F. *Arms and Insecurity*, Pittsburgh: Boxwood, 1960.

Romer, Paul M. "Endogenous Technological Change," *Journal of Political Economy*, 98:5 (October 1990), pp. 71–102.

Romer, Paul M. "Increasing Returns and Long-Run Growth," *Journal of Political Economy*, 94:5 (October 1986), pp. 1002–1037.

Scales, MG Robert H., Jr. *Future Warfare*, Carlisle Barracks, PA: U.S. Army War College, 1999.

Schulze, Guenther G., and Heinrich W. Ursprung. "Globalisation of the Economy and the Nation State," *The World Economy*, 22:3 (May 1999), pp. 295–352.

Schweller, Randall L. "Bandwagoning for Profit: Bringing the Revisionist State Back In," *International Security*, 19:1 (Summer 1994), pp. 72–107.

Schweller, Randall. "Domestic Structure and Preventive War: Are Democracies More Pacific?" *World Politics*, 44:2 (January 1992), pp. 235–269.

Schweller, Randall L. "Tripolarity and the Second World War," *International Studies Quarterly*, 37:1 (March 1993), pp. 73–103.

Schweller, Randall L., and William C. Wohlforth. "Power Test: Evaluating Realism in Response to the End of the Cold War," *Security Studies*, 9:3 (Spring 2000), pp. 60–107.

Shapiro, Jeremy. "Information and War," in Zalmay Khalilzad, John P. White, and Andrew W. Marshall, *Strategic Appraisal: The Changing Role of Information in Warfare*, Santa Monica, CA: RAND, MR-1016-AF, 1999, pp. 113–154.

Siverson, Randolph M. "Democracies and War Participation: In Defense of the Institutional Constraints Argument," *European Journal of International Relations*, 1 (December 1995), pp. 481–490.

Skocpol, Theda. "Social Revolutions and Mass Military Mobilization," *World Politics*, 40:2 (January 1988), pp. 147–168.

Snyder, Glenn H. *Alliance Politics*, Ithaca, NY: Cornell University Press, 1997.

Snyder, Glenn H., "Alliances, Balance, and Stability," *International Organization*, 45:1 (Winter 1991), pp. 121–142.

Snyder, Jack L. *From Voting to Violence: Democratization and National Conflict*, New York: W. W Norton, 2000.

Spiro, David E. "The Insignificance of the Liberal Peace," *International Security*, 19:2 (Fall 1994), pp. 50–86.

Swaine, Michael D., and Ashley J. Tellis. *Interpreting China's Grand Strategy*, Santa Monica, CA: RAND, 2000.

Tammen, Ronald L., Jacek Kugler, Douglas Lemke, Allan C. Stam III, Mark Abdollahian, Carole Alsharabati, Brian Efird, and A.F.K. Organski. *Power Transitions: Strategies for the 21st Century*, New York and London: Chatham House Publishers, 2000.

Tangredi, Sam J. *All Possible Wars? Toward a Consensus View of the Future Security Environment, 2001–2025*, McNair Paper 63, Washington, D.C.: Institute for National Strategic Studies, National Defense University, 2000.

Tellis, Ashley J., Janice Bially, Christopher Layne, Melissa McPherson. *Measuring National Power in the Postindustrial Age*, Santa Monica, CA: RAND, MR-1110-A, 2000.

Thompson, William R. "Principal Rivalries," *Journal of Conflict Resolution*, 39:2 (June 1995), pp. 195–223.

Thompson, William R., and Richard Tucker. "A Tale of Two Democratic Peace Critiques," *Journal of Conflict Resolution*, 41:3 (June 1997), pp. 428–454.

Trimberger, Ellen Kay. *Revolution from Above: Military Bureaucrats and Development in Japan, Turkey, Egypt, and Peru*, New Brunswick, NJ: Transaction Books, 1978.

Van Evera, Stephen. "Primed for Peace," *International Security*, 15:3 (Winter 1990/91), pp. 7–57.

Vasquez, John A. *The War Puzzle*, Cambridge: Cambridge University Press, 1993.

Walt, Stephen M., *Revolution and War*, Ithaca, NY: Cornell University Press, 1996.

Walt, Stephen M. *The Origins of Alliances*, Ithaca, NY: Cornell University Press, 1987.

Waltz, Kenneth N. "Structural Realism After the Cold War," *International Security*, 25:1 (Summer 2000), pp. 5–41.

Waltz, Kenneth. *Theory of International Politics*, Reading, MA: Addison-Wesley, 1979.

Ward, Michael D., and Kristian S. Gleditsch. "Democratizing for Peace," *American Political Science Review*, 92:1 (March 1998), pp. 51–61.

Weiss, Linda. *The Myth of the Powerless State*, Ithaca, NY: Cornell University Press, 1998.

Weyland, Kurt. "Risk Taking in Latin American Economic Restructuring: Lessons from Prospect Theory," *International Studies Quarterly*, 40:2 (June 1996), pp. 185–208.

Wohlforth, William C. "The Stability of a Unipolar World," *International Security*, 24:1 (Summer 1999), pp. 28–31.

Wolf, Reinhard, Erich Weede, Andrew J. Enterline, and Edward D. Mansfield and Jack Snyder. "Correspondence: Democratization and the Danger of War," *International Security*, 20:4 (Spring 1996), pp. 176–207.

World Bank, *The East Asian Miracle: Economic Growth and Public Policy*, New York: Oxford University Press, 1993.

Zakaria, Fareed. *From Wealth to Power: The Unusual Origins of America's World Role*, Princeton, NJ: Princeton University Press, 1999.